ALL MADDEN

ALSO BY JOHN MADDEN WITH DAVE ANDERSON
Hey, Wait a Minute (I Wrote a Book!)
One Knee Equals Two Feet
(And Everything Else You Need to Know About Football)
One Size Doesn't Fit All

ALSO BY JOHN MADDEN
My First Football Book
Inside Madden '94

ALSO BY DAVE ANDERSON
Pennant Races
In the Corner
Sports of Our Times
Countdown to Super Bowl
Always on the Run (with Larry Csonka and Jim Kiick)
Sugar Ray (with Sugar Ray Robinson)
Shooting for the Gold
Frank: The First Year (with Frank Robinson)
The Yankees
Upset
Return of a Champion: Pancho Gonzalez
The Story of the Olympics
The Story of Football
The Story of Basketball
Great Quarterbacks of the NFL
Great Pass-Receivers of the NFL
Great Defensive Players of the NFL

ALL MADDEN

Hey, I'm Talking Pro Football!

JOHN MADDEN
WITH DAVE ANDERSON

HarperCollins*Publishers*

HarperCollins books may be purchased for educational, business, or sales promotional use. For information please write: Special Markets Department, HarperCollins Publishers, Inc., 10 East 53rd Street, New York, NY 10022.

FIRST EDITION

Designed by Laura Lindgren

Library of Congress Cataloging-in-Publication Data

Madden, John, 1936–
    All Madden / John Madden with Dave Anderson. — 1st ed.
        p.   cm.
    ISBN 0-06-017205-3
    1. Madden, John, 1936–   . 2. Sportscasters—United States—Biography. 3. Football coaches—United States—Biography. 4. Football—United States—Miscellanea. 5. Football players—Rating of—United States. I. Anderson, Dave. II. Title.
GV742.42.M33A33   1996
070.4'49796'092—dc20
[B]
                                                                96-23325

96 97 98 99 00 ❖/RRD 10 9 8 7 6 5 4 3 2 1

CONTENTS

ALL MADDEN

BACK TO
THE SUPER BOWL

In my travels, people usually ask me two questions. The first is, "Where's your bus?" The other is, "Who's going to win the Super Bowl?"

I always know where my bus is parked, but I never know which team is going to win the Super Bowl. I start getting that question in the off-season, then I keep getting it during the preseason, the regular season, and the play-offs—right up to the Super Bowl itself. But I'm not very good at knowing which team is going to win. I'm a firm believer that things change, that teams get better or worse, that key players get hurt, that a team has to do it on the field. But when I tell people I don't know who's going to win, they just look at me.

"John Madden, you know football," they'll say. "You know who's going to win."

Hey, I really don't know. I might think one team will win, but I don't *know* it will. That's the great thing about the Super Bowl game and most NFL games. If it ever got to the point where you and I always knew which team was going to win before they played, it wouldn't be a game.

When you think about it, the Super Bowl itself is like that. No one knew it would be what it is now—the world's biggest one-day sports event.

When it started, when Vince Lombardi's Packers beat the Chiefs, 35–10, on January 15, 1967, in the Los Angeles Memorial Coliseum, its official name was the AFL–NFL World Championship Game. Not until the Jets–Colts game in January 1969 did the cover of the game program use the term *Super Bowl,* which was Lamar Hunt's nickname for the game after watching his daughter Sharon play with a high-bouncing ball.

"What kind of ball is that?" Lamar asked.

"It's called the Super Ball," she said.

Before that first game, Lamar Hunt, the owner of the Chiefs, suggested it be called the Super Bowl, but it didn't catch on then, maybe because the NFL owners didn't think the game would be super. They thought the American Football League was inferior. They had agreed to the 1966 merger to control their payrolls, to stop players from jumping from one league to another, and to create a common draft that would stop the bidding for the best players coming out of college.

What the Super Bowl has become reminds me of a conversation I once had with Jack Nicklaus while doing a CBS special.

"Naming your first son Jack II," I said, "didn't that put a lot of pressure on him, just having to live with the name Jack Nicklaus after all you've done in golf?"

"When I named him Jack Nicklaus II," Jack said, "I didn't know I was going to be Jack Nicklaus."

He's considered the best golfer in history now but when his son was born in 1961, Jack Nicklaus was still an amateur. He turned pro the next year and won the U.S. Open, the first of his record eighteen major championships. What's happened with the Super Bowl is something like that. When it started, we didn't know it was going to be Jack

Nicklaus. We didn't know it was going to be the Super Bowl.

We didn't know that Super Bowl XXX in Phoenix was going to be one big celebration—the commissioner's party, the NFL Properties party, the NFL Experience, and the NFL players' party, not to mention more than four dozen other functions and all the media coverage.

At the 1997 game in New Orleans, I'll be doing my first Super Bowl for the Fox Television Network, my eighth as either a broadcaster or a coach. I can appreciate the Super Bowl's growth because I remember what it was like in January 1968 at Super Bowl II in Miami, the end of my first season as a Raiders assistant coach. We had routed the Oilers, 40–7, in Oakland for the AFL championship after the Packers had edged the Cowboys, 21–17, on Bart Starr's quarterback sneak in minus-thirteen-degree weather in Green Bay, the NFL title game now known as the Ice Bowl.

I look now at all the Super Bowl news conferences and functions, but there wasn't much of that then. We stayed in the University Inn motel in Boca Raton and practiced at a little prep school there. The writers mostly stayed in Miami hotels. If any of them wanted to talk to a Raiders player, they drove up and knocked on the door of his hotel room.

The only party I remember was Commissioner Pete Rozelle's little party for maybe two hundred pro-football people and writers Friday night at the Doral Hotel in Miami Beach. I drove down there with the other assistant coaches. Walking in, the first guy I saw was Pat Summerall, who was there to do the game for CBS as one of its analysts. I introduced myself and we talked a little. Thirteen years later we would begin sharing a television broadcast booth at NFL games and we've been sharing one ever since, most recently for Fox.

But for me, the biggest thrill of that Super Bowl was just being on the Raiders sideline in the Orange Bowl across from Vince Lombardi, who was coaching his last game for the Packers.

As a young coach, I idolized Vince Lombardi. I always thought that if I were going to be a head coach, I'd have to do it the way he did. Start out as a high-school coach, then be a college assistant coach, then a pro assistant coach, then probably take over a team that was down because no team that was up needed a head coach. When he took over the Packers in 1959, they had been down, but he built them into the NFL champions of 1961, 1962, 1965, 1966, and 1967.

Once, between plays in Super Bowl II, I looked over and just watched Vince Lombardi standing there in his blue blazer, white shirt, red-and-blue-striped tie, gray slacks, and black football shoes with white laces. I thought, *I'm on this sideline and Vince Lombardi is on the other sideline. I'm telling my linebackers how to stop Vince Lombardi's plays.*

To me, that was almost like trying to stop God's plays. And that's about how effective we were. We lost, 33–14. We fell behind, 13–0, before Daryle Lamonica hit Bill Miller with a 23-yard touchdown pass. Just before halftime the Packers' left-footed Donny Anderson hung a punt. Roger Bird called for a fair catch near midfield, but fumbled. The Packers recovered at our 45-yard line with twenty-three seconds remaining. Instead of us having a chance for George Blanda to kick a field goal that would have made it 13–10, the Packers' Don Chandler kicked a 43-yard field goal for a 16–7 lead. In the second half, the Packers opened it to 33–7 before Daryle Lamonica threw another touchdown pass to Bill Miller.

That fumbled punt stayed with me. Whenever the Raiders played a team with a left-footed punter after that, I always made sure our punt returner caught some punts from a left-footed punter in practice. The flight of a football can be compared to that of a golf ball. A left-hander's hook resembles a right-hander's slice, and vice versa.

But something else stayed with Al Treml, the Packers' film director then and now. When I sent him an All-

Madden sweatshirt for helping us with the 1995 *All-Madden* television show, he sent me a note. "Thanks for the sweatshirt," he wrote, "but it doesn't make up for sending the films late before Super Bowl II."

I wasn't just the linebacker coach then. I was also in charge of the film exchange. At the start of the season, I didn't know the games that coaches like Sid Gillman, Weeb Ewbank, and Hank Stram played with films. The first few weeks that season, I sent on Monday the films of our last two games to our next opponent. In return, they were supposed to send films of *their* last two games. But our opponents' films seldom arrived.

"Where are the films?" the other coaches would ask.

"I don't know," I'd say. "They're not here yet."

After that happened a few times, I decided not to send our films until we got our opponents' films. So before that Super Bowl with the Packers, I didn't send our films to Green Bay until we got their films. Vince Lombardi complained, just like the AFL coaches had complained, but that was the great thing about working for Al Davis, the Raiders' managing general partner who had been the AFL commissioner at the time of the merger. Nobody in the NFL or the AFL trusted Al to play by the rules. When our films didn't arrive, other teams always blamed Al, not me.

"John, we know it's not you, we know it's Al," one of the other team's assistant coaches would say to me. "But we need those films."

I'd say, "Yeah, they're on the way." Sometimes they were, as long as I already had their films. But at the time of that Super Bowl II loss, everybody on the Raiders thought we would be back next year, if not every year. It didn't turn out that way. In 1968 we didn't get to Super Bowl III because we lost the AFC championship game to the Jets, 27–23, in Shea Stadium. When the Jets beat the Baltimore Colts, 16–7, we had wanted them to win for the AFL's sake, but we didn't celebrate the Jets' victory. We were still down not only from not getting to the Super Bowl ourselves but from knowing we would've beaten the Colts if we had.

The next year, my first as the Raiders' head coach, the same thing happened. We had beaten the Chiefs three times, twice in the regular season and once in the pre-season. But when the Chiefs beat us, 17–7, in the AFL championship game in Oakland, they went to Super Bowl IV and beat the Vikings, 23–7. Once again, we were down not only from not getting to the Super Bowl ourselves but from knowing we would've beaten the Vikings if we had.

That's the tough thing about the playoffs. No matter how many teams make the playoffs, every one but one is going to lose its last game. When you lose your last game in the playoffs, you have your whole off-season to think about it. That happened to the Raiders again in 1970, 1972, 1973, 1974, and 1975 before we beat the Steelers, 24–7, to get to Super Bowl XI against the Vikings in the Rose Bowl. By then the Super Bowl was evolving into what it is now. Everyone wanted tickets. All those morning news conferences for the coaches and players. More and more parties.

In reading about previous Super Bowl weeks, I had noticed that the teams that complained about distractions invariably lost. I'd also noticed that some players in other sports seemed to freeze up before championship games, as if they had the weight of the world on their shoulders. I wanted my players to enjoy getting ready.

"If we're going to win this thing, if this is going to be something we'll remember the rest of our lives, then let's act like it is," I told my players in our first Super Bowl meeting. "Someday you're going to be in a rocking chair rocking a grandchild and telling that little boy or little girl about winning Super Bowl XI and being a world champion, about the big diamond ring, and about how that was the greatest day of your football life, so make it the greatest day. We're not going to complain about anything down there. We're going to work hard. We're going to study. We're going to prepare in practice. We're going to win. And we're going to enjoy it too."

But the Wednesday before the game I wasn't enjoying it. Wednesday we always majored in defense with a little offense thrown in. Thursday we majored in offense with a little defense thrown in. But after that Wednesday practice, I went on a tirade.

We'd had a sloppy practice. Too many mistakes. Someone would miss a call or jump offside. It wasn't an attitude thing. It wasn't anything someone did or said. It was just too many mistakes. I hated mistakes. Back in the locker room I ranted and raved.

Thursday we worked on offense, mostly throwing the ball. We threw it without any defense, then just against the defensive backs, then with seven on seven, then with eleven on eleven. Earlier that week it had rained, so our practice field at the University of California at Irvine was still a little slick and the weather forecast for that afternoon was for rain, so I made sure we had extra footballs out there. I never wanted my quarterback to throw a wet ball. I didn't want it to be heavy. I didn't want his hand to slip and put pressure on his elbow. I always wanted him to be throwing a dry ball, so we had towel guys all over the place. Any time a ball hit the ground, they were to pick it up and wipe it off, then dry it off. If there was a smudge on it, they were to throw it in the ball bag.

As it turned out, it didn't rain during that practice, but Ken Stabler threw more than a hundred passes and only one ball hit the ground. One pass sailed over tight end Dave Casper's head. Every other ball was caught.

We'd had the closest thing to a perfect practice that I ever experienced as a coach, or have ever observed as a broadcaster. As angry as I had been the day before, I was that confident now. Walking off the field and through a gate to our locker room, I remember thinking, *We're there now. This team is just where you want it. Just don't screw it up because that's the only way we can lose. Don't do something stupid. Don't work 'em too hard tomorrow or run 'em too hard on Saturday. Just keep this train rolling.* We didn't do much the next two days, just enough to keep them loose. Saturday night I was talking to Al Davis.

"There's no way we can lose," I said.

"Don't say that," Al said. "Don't jinx us."

"But there's no way we can lose," I said.

As a coach, I never went into any other game so sure that we'd win. And we did, 32–14. We were the Super Bowl champions. Then as now, that's really what you play for in the NFL. Players can talk about who's the highest paid, about how much money they make, about how many touchdown passes they've thrown, about how many times they've rushed for a thousand yards or caught passes for a thousand yards, about how many sacks they have, about how many Pro Bowl teams they've been on, but it's still all about winning the Super Bowl.

But even when the Raiders won Super Bowl XI, the meaning didn't really sink in until a few weeks later at the Washington (D.C.) Touchdown Club dinner when Roger Staubach came up to me.

"Congratulations, John," he said. "Now that you've won the Super Bowl, they can never take that away from you. They can never say again that you can't win the big one."

And we won it while enjoying the week. I think our approach carried over to the Raiders who won Super Bowl XV from the Eagles. Tom Flores had succeeded me in 1979 as the Raiders' coach, but he had been on my staff for seven seasons. He knew our approach to Super Bowl XI had helped us win. The week of Super Bowl XV in New Orleans, I was working for CBS Radio and I remember thinking that the Raiders were enjoying being there but the Eagles weren't. The Raiders won, 27–10.

The next year, Super Bowl XVI, was the first time the game was scheduled in the North, in the Pontiac Silverdome near Detroit. Outside the weather was cold with snow and ice, but everyone had a good time. I thought the 49ers enjoyed it more than the Bengals did. Bill Walsh certainly did. As the 49ers' coach, he was an intense guy but when the 49ers' buses arrived Sunday night at their hotel in the Detroit suburbs, they were greeted by a silver-haired bellman.

"Help you with your bag?" the bellman asked.

At first the players ignored him, then one of the 49ers recognized the bellman—Bill Walsh, their coach. Bill laughed about that all week. His players did too. Players like their young quarterback, Joe Montana, and their rookie defensive back, Ronnie Lott.

Those laughs had to help the 49ers win, 26–21, but in my first Super Bowl in the booth with Pat Summerall for CBS television, I wasn't laughing. I had made a rookie mistake.

In our CBS openings during the season and the playoff games, when Pat and I talked briefly about the game, each of us held a hand microphone instead of using the microphone attached to the headset we wore during the game. Sometimes we did the opening standing up, sometimes sitting in a chair. But in the booth at the Silverdome that day we did it sitting on our worktable that holds the monitors and stuff. We opened with both of us on camera together, then Pat said something and I talked about it, then he said something else and I talked about it. But while I was talking the second time, the camera zoomed in on me so Pat could put down his hand microphone and put on his headset. Then when I was done, they would get pictures of the field and Pat would start talking.

Anyway, there I was, sitting on the table, finishing up the opening for my first Super Bowl on television, but Pat was just standing there to the side.

Instead of having his headset on, he was looking around for it. When I finished what I had to say, there was just silence on the air. Pat was still looking around for his headset. I finally stood up. I had been sitting on Pat's headset but never realized it. Now that's a test of friendship. But as Pat stood there, he had figured out where his headset had to be. As cool as ever, he waited until I stood up, then reached over, picked up his headset, put it on, adjusted it, and started talking. I don't know how long the silence on the air had lasted, but to me it had seemed like an eternity.

Three years later, at Super Bowl XVIII in Tampa, the Raiders against the Redskins, I made sure I didn't sit on Pat's headset. By then, having been with CBS for five seasons and doing more NFC games than AFC games, I knew the Redskins better than I did the Raiders.

The Raiders won, 38–9, in a game that was over just before halftime. The Redskins were backed up on their own 12-yard line when Joe Theismann threw a screen pass that Raiders linebacker Jack Squirek intercepted and ran in for a 21–3 lead. We were staying at the Bay Harbor Inn, where the Raiders were staying, and most people probably thought I was talking to Al Davis all week. But we were coming and going at different times. I didn't talk to him until a few hours after the game. I was in the lobby, he walked in, and I congratulated him.

Three years later, we did Super Bowl XXI, the Giants against the Broncos in the Rose Bowl.

During that week the Giants practiced at the Rams complex in Anaheim where all they seemed to be worrying about, especially Lawrence Taylor, was how to throw or kick a tennis ball past a big dog who stood in a doorway of the locker room like a hockey goalie. The dog's name was Ofor.

"When a dog goes into the pound," somebody on the Rams explained to me that week, "if nobody adopts the dog in five days, they put him to sleep. This dog was oh for four when we took him on the fifth day, so we named him Ofor."

During practice L.T. couldn't wait to get back to the locker room to try to get the ball past that big dog, who had some German shepherd in him but was as quick as a cat. I don't know if L.T. ever got the ball past him, but he and all the Giants just loved that dog. They also loved the perfect weather, sunny and warm, but their coach didn't.

"Now I know why the Rams don't win here," Bill Parcells told me. "It's too nice. Nobody wants to play."

The Giants had just beaten the Redskins, 17–0, in the NFC championship game in Giants Stadium in weather that Bill loved—windy bone-chilling cold. He's a Jersey guy who grew up in that weather. He wanted that weather. He put the Giants together to play in that weather. But in that same perfect weather in the Rose Bowl on Sunday his quarterback, Phil Simms, had a virtually perfect game. He completed twenty-two of twenty-five passes for 268 yards and three touchdowns as the Giants won, 39–20, in a game Pat and I almost didn't get to.

That was the year before I had my bus. Sandy Montag, my agent at the International Management Group, was driving me up from Los Angeles to Pasadena in a van, and Pat Summerall was in a car following us.

We were supposed to get off the freeway at a certain exit where a police car would be waiting to escort us through the Rose Bowl traffic. I had been reading the Sunday papers, not paying any attention to where we were, but when I looked at my watch I knew we should be close to Pasadena.

"How far is Pasadena?" I asked.

"We missed it," Sandy said.

"How could we miss Pasadena!"

We not only had missed our exit, but by now we also had missed all the Rose Bowl exits and we had missed all the Pasadena exits.

"Our biggest game of the year," I roared, "and you not only miss the exit for the stadium but miss the exit for the town."

The car Pat was in had followed us and missed it too.

At the next exit, Sandy got off and we came back down the freeway to the first Rose Bowl exit we saw. It was still about three hours before the game, but the traffic was building up. Luckily, we spotted an ambulance that was going to the Rose Bowl where it would park in case it was needed. Sandy got behind that ambulance, Pat's car got behind us, and we followed that ambulance to our parking lot.

Three years later, at Super Bowl XXIV, the 49ers against the Broncos, we didn't have to worry about getting to the game. In New Orleans the downtown hotels are only a few blocks from the Superdome.

That week I remember going to a Broncos practice, then going to a 49ers practice, back to back, and thinking, *There's no way the Broncos can win.* The 49ers were too quick, too talented. That's when I realized that what made the 49ers so good was their ability to get off first. That's a boxing term. You'll hear a boxing trainer tell his fighter, "Get off first, throw your jab before the other guy throws his." In football, that's what the 49ers were doing in practice that day, just like they had done it to other teams during the season.

Except for when I knew my 1976 Raiders would win Super Bowl XI, the way I felt about the 49ers before Super Bowl XXIV was the closest I've ever been to knowing a pro football team would win.

After that 49ers practice, we drove Joe Montana back to his hotel. He was the same Joe Montana I'd known, talking football, joking around. But it was like having a rock star on the bus. He had two security guards with him, and we couldn't just drop him off at the front door. We had to drive around to the kitchen door where crates of lettuce were piled up. He disappeared past the lettuce and rode the room-service elevator to his floor. The next day he threw five touchdown passes as the 49ers won, 55–10.

Two years later, the Redskins against the Bills in Super Bowl XXVI, we were in Minneapolis where it was so cold, we went ice fishing with some of our CBS crew.

I'd always wondered why people ice-fished, and I found out. It's just getting out of the house in the winter and sitting on the ice and talking. It's just camaraderie. We rode the bus for two hours up to a frozen lake where a guy drilled holes in the ice with a machine. Some of the regulars there ice-fished from inside a shed, but we wanted to fish outside. We were sitting on little chairs out there on the ice, all bundled up, trying to keep warm, watching our line bob in the water, when a guy carrying portable heaters walked over to the only woman with us, Lesley Visser.

"Want a heater?" he asked.

"Of course not," she said.

All us guys were freezing but when Lesley turned down the heater, now all us machos had to turn down the heater whether we wanted to or not. In fact, the guy with the heaters asked me next.

"No," I said, "I don't need a heater."

I never caught any fish, but some of the CBS guys got some walleyes and northern pike. On our way back to Minneapolis in the bus, Lance Barrow, who is now a golf producer for CBS, cooked all the fish. Best fish I've ever had. Talk about fresh fish, that fish was just minutes out of a lake. That fish was also better than the game. The Redskins were bigger and better. They won, 37–24, after Thurman Thomas, the Bills' running back, missed the first few plays when he couldn't find his helmet.

The way the television rotation worked out, that was my last Super Bowl for CBS, and now Super Bowl XXXI will be my first for Fox, which really makes it special.

Wherever I go now, some people will tell me, "I hope you get a good matchup. I hope you get a good game." But I really never worry about that. You can't control the matchup. You can't control the game. All we can do is cover the game. It doesn't make any difference what teams you might want in the Super Bowl, it's what teams deserve to be there by getting there. That's the matchup. And the game is however those two teams play.

Another thing some people tell me is, "I hope you don't get a boring game."

But even when the Super Bowl is one-sided, not everybody is bored. When I was the Raiders' coach in Super Bowl XI and we won big, some people probably thought it was boring, but it wasn't boring to us. It's the biggest game of the year and if you're the coach and your team is winning big, believe me, you're happy and your players are happy and your fans are happy. If you want to win and you're winning, it's not boring.

Whatever happens, I'm just glad I'll be doing the Super Bowl again. If you're involved in pro football, at the end of the season the Super Bowl is where you want to be.

2

IT'S LIKE
I'M STILL A KID

When I was growing up in Daly City, just over the San Francisco line, John Robinson was one of my best friends and he still is. He's the football coach at Southern California now after having been the Los Angeles Rams' coach for nine seasons. To me, it's just amazing that two NFL coaches could come out of the same neighborhood where they played football, baseball, and basketball when they weren't talking about sports like kids do.

"I'm Ted Williams," John would say when we were playing baseball, meaning the Boston Red Sox slugger.

"I'm Bob Toneff," I would say when we were playing football, meaning the 49ers' All-Pro tackle of that era.

When we were talking about boxing, John would put his hands up and say, "I'm Sugar Ray Robinson," because they had the same last name. But sometimes we'd get into a debate, and one of us would say, "I'll bet you a million dollars" about something when neither of us had a nickel. Another thing we were always telling each other was, "You know what you oughta do, you oughta . . ."

Then one day in 1984 when John Robinson was coaching the Rams and I was in my sixth year doing NFL games on television after ten seasons as the Oakland Raiders' coach, we were talking.

"You know what you oughta do?" he said to me. "You oughta pick your own All-NFL team with your guys on it. Not an All-Pro team. Just the players who are your kind of guys."

I liked the idea, but the guy who really liked it was Terry O'Neil, then our CBS executive producer. He even had the name, the All-Madden team. And now the title of this book is *All Madden* (without the hyphen). This book is all about pro football and its players and coaches and owners as I've seen them and known them, not what may occur in their lives away from football. It's also about broadcasting, about what I do and how I do it. To me, it's like I'm still a kid. I'm having as much fun now as I did then. Maybe more. I do NFL games for Fox Television. I ride my Madden Cruiser bus all over America to get to those games. I do a Monday-to-Friday morning radio show on KNBR in San Francisco. I've got a football video game, Madden NFL 97 from Electronic Arts. I do television commercials for Ace Hardware, Sony, Outback Steakhouse, and Tinactin.

The best part is, as busy as I am, I never feel like I'm really working. I'm just having a good time doing what I did as a kid. Going to football games and talking about them. Talking about sports. I've always believed that if you're having a good time, you might have a job but it's not really work.

My philosophy is that football is a game, and if it's a game, it should be fun. Basically the guys on my annual All-Madden team are those who have fun playing the game. Some are the same guys who go to the Pro Bowl every year, like Jerry Rice and Emmitt Smith, but some aren't even in their team's starting lineup, like Bill Bates, who's on the Cowboys' special teams. Some don't get as much mention as they should for being good football players. And if they get a little more mud on their uniforms than most guys, all the better. The guys on the team get an All-Madden jacket and a gray sweatshirt with our leather-helmet logo. The sweatshirt has to be gray, because years ago that was the only color sweatshirts came in.

They're all players who would be fun to coach, fun to have on a team. They also have to be players I saw play that season. That means they're mostly National Conference players because Fox televises mostly National Conference teams.

I'd like to have more American Conference players, but I don't want to go by what other people tell me, by what highlights I see, or by what I read in the papers. If I don't see someone actually play in a game that season, I don't put him on the team. Except once. I didn't see Joe Montana play in 1993 with the Chiefs, but I put him on anyway.

Hey, this was Joe Montana. I had seen him all those years when he was with the 49ers, I didn't have to see him in a Chiefs uniform. I knew he was the same Joe Montana.

I take the All-Madden team very seriously, but some players take it even more seriously. Especially if they don't make it. When Sterling Sharpe was a wide receiver for the Packers, he actually went to court to get his name changed legally.

"I knew that with a name like Sterling, I'd never make the All-Madden team," he said, "so I said, 'Judge, I want to change my name to Dirt.'"

He was joking. He made the team as Sterling Sharpe, twice. But when I visited the Vikings complex in 1995, Cris Carter wasn't joking. I was talking to linebacker Jack Del Rio when Cris stopped, looked at Jack, and then pointed to me.

"Don't talk to this man," Cris said. "I had one hundred twenty-two catches last year, an all-time NFL record, and he didn't put me on his All-Madden team. One hundred twenty-two catches!"

He was serious. When he caught another 122 passes in 1995, he was on it. Then there was the time I was talking to Daryl Johnston's mother. She does a newsletter known as *The Moose Call* about her son, the Cowboys fullback whose blocking helps open the holes Emmitt Smith runs through.

"You had Daryl on your 1992 team," she said, "but you haven't put him on since."

"I put Daryl on that year," I said, "because he was doing all that great blocking and not getting much credit for it. When he made the Pro Bowl the next two years, he was no longer underrated so I didn't have to put him on."

"That's what I thought," she said.

There's an All-Madden Haul of Fame too, and that's not a typo. Haul of Fame is correct. *H-a-u-l*, not *h-a-l-l*. Because there is no hall. I just haul a big ol' wooden plaque around the country on my bus that Willie Yarborough and Dave Hahn drive, then I put that same big ol' plaque up at one of my favorite places every year and induct some of my favorite players.

The first year, 1991, I put that plaque up in Chuy's (pronounced *Chewey's*), a Mexican restaurant in Van Horn, Texas, on the dusty plains off Interstate 10 not far from El Paso. The last time we went through there, the population was 2,861, up a few from 1987 when we first stopped there.

On the way from Tampa to Anaheim that year, we were looking for a place to eat where we could also watch the Monday night game. Coming into Van Horn, we saw a sign that said, "Mexican Food" and "TV Room." What a discovery. Not only was there a big-screen television, but Chuy Uranga and his wife, Mary Lou, made the best tamales I've ever had. Not that fancy Mexican stuff and foamy margaritas you get in those trendy places. Just real food and real beer. Ever since that Monday night we always stop at Chuy's whenever we go through Van Horn around lunchtime or dinnertime. The room where we eat is now the "John Madden Room," and there's a chair with my name on it and chairs for my sons, Mike and Joe, and my drivers, Willie and Dave, with their names on them. Chuy's was the perfect place to put up that big ol' plaque for the first Haul of Fame inductees: Bears linebacker Mike Singletary and Bengals offensive tackle Anthony Munoz.

In 1992 we stopped in Medicine Bow, Wyoming, and hung offensive tackle Joe Jacoby's big Redskins jersey in the Virginian Hotel. The next year we put Giants linebacker Lawrence Taylor's jersey in a truck stop in Greenville, Illinois; then in 1995, on a cobblestone street under the Brooklyn Bridge, we inducted Joe Montana, 49ers safety Ronnie Lott, and Rams offensive tackle Jackie Slater.

In the opening for that first All-Madden show in 1984, I said, "This team doesn't make a lot of sense. They have All-America teams, All-Pro teams, Pro Bowl teams, and all those make sense. This doesn't. This is just a bunch of guys that we've seen, that we've met, that we've watched play, that we've admired. I thought it would be kind of fun to just put 'em all together." It's been so much fun, that for this book I've put together an All-Time All-Madden team of players I've seen since 1979 when I began broadcasting NFL games.

QUARTERBACK: Joe Montana

RUNNING BACKS: Walter Payton, John Riggins, Barry Sanders, Emmitt Smith

WIDE RECEIVERS: Jerry Rice, Gary Clark

TIGHT END: Mark Bavaro

OFFENSIVE LINEMEN: Joe Jacoby, Jackie Slater, Anthony Munoz, Jay Hilgenberg, Nate Newton, Russ Grimm

DEFENSIVE LINEMEN: Reggie White, Charles Haley, Howie Long, Jack Youngblood, Jim Burt, Richard Dent

LINEBACKERS: Lawrence Taylor, Mike Singletary, Matt Millen, Rickey Jackson

DEFENSIVE BACKS: Ronnie Lott, Mike Haynes, Darrell Green, Lester Hayes

SPECIAL TEAMS: Bill Bates, Jan Stenerud, Pat Summerall (always)

Of all those players, I think Jack Youngblood, a defensive end for the Rams in Los Angeles and Anaheim, personified the All-Madden team spirit when he suffered a broken lower left leg near the end of the first half of a 1979 playoff game against the Cowboys in Texas Stadium. He tells the story better than anyone.

"They took me into the locker room," Jack says, "took an X ray, looked at it, and said, 'That's what we expected, a broken fibula.'

"I said, 'Okay, tape it up.'

"They said, 'No, no, you don't understand. You can't tape a broken leg.'

"I said, 'Yeah, you can. Tape it up. Tape two aspirin to it, and let's go. This is the divisional playoff. Tape it. Let's play. Let's go do it.'"

The doctors taped him up.

Jack Youngblood finished that game, played the NFC championship game in Tampa the next week, then played against the Steelers in Super Bowl XIV two weeks later. All on a broken leg that he says took longer to heal than usual but otherwise had no lasting effect.

"The pain was like having a knife stuck in the side of your leg constantly, but it was absolutely worth it," Jack says. "You cannot miss an opportunity to play in the Super Bowl."

Ronnie Lott had that same spirit. When he tackled Cowboys running back Tim Newsome in the 49ers' season finale in 1985, his left pinky was smashed between his helmet and Tim's chest. From the base of the nail to the tip, his finger was a mess, but the 49ers had a wild-card playoff in Giants Stadium the following Sunday.

"The doctor told me, 'You can't play,'" Ronnie remembers, "but I told him, 'I'm playing.'"

"He said, 'You lost a piece of the bone.'

"But I said, 'Fix it up so I can play.'"

Ronnie played, but the 49ers lost, 17–3. About a month

later his finger still hadn't healed. He was given a choice, either amputate the tip of the pinky or do a bone graft. He chose amputation. But the next season he was an All-Pro and All-Madden safety. While finishing his career in 1994 with the Jets, he was named to the NFL's seventy-fifth anniversary team.

"It's still a little sensitive," he says of his pinky, "but so what."

I'm not recommending that your son or your nephew do that in Pop Warner football or even high school or college football. But in the NFL every team needs players who would do that. Usually they're big strong guys like Jack Youngblood or Ronnie Lott, but sometimes little guys are just as tough. Maybe even tougher in their own way, like Gary Clark, who was on two Super Bowl championship teams with the Redskins.

Gary is only five feet nine but he's just one of those guys, whatever you want to do, you would want him with you. Play football. Climb a mountain. Dig a foxhole. All he wants to do is win.

Some players always look neat and clean, but Gary always had stuff flopping on his uniform, mud on his face, grass in the ear hole of his helmet. When he got knocked down, he hopped right up and ran back to the huddle. Sometimes he'd be so beat up, he couldn't practice all week but on Sunday he'd catch eight passes, score two touchdowns, and win the game. To me, he always personified what a pro football player should be. Compete. Play to win. Fight and scrap.

Football players are my guys, but every so often I put people on the All-Madden team who are not players, like Ernie Palladino, the little New York sportswriter who stood up to Lawrence Taylor.

When the Giants were struggling during the 1995 season, Lawrence Taylor, the linebacker who was All-Madden eight times, stopped by one day to talk to the team, then went out to watch practice. Ernie Palladino, who covers the Giants for the Gannett suburban newspapers, asked L.T. to tell the writers what he had told the team, but L.T. declined. With that, Ernie and L.T. got into what you might call a debate that escalated into L.T. grabbing Ernie by the throat. Ernie is five feet five and a half, 162 pounds, L.T. is six three and 240, but the mismatch was quickly broken up. In apologizing later, L.T. handed Ernie his 1993 All-Madden leather jacket.

"You deserve this," L.T. said with a smile, "because you're crazier than I am."

Ernie handed the jacket to Pat Hanlon, the Giants' public-relations director.

"I can't keep this," Ernie said. "It's yours to do whatever you want to do with it."

Pat Hanlon decided to auction L.T.'s leather jacket for the Giants Academy, part of the Newark, New Jersey, inner-city public school system. At a telephone auction on WOR's pregame radio show in October, it brought a $3,000 bid from a woman named Ronney Rosenberg, a Citibank oil and gas stock trader. When I got to Giants Stadium a few weeks later, I presented it to her on the pregame radio show.

"This is a very special jacket," I said. "And what a great way to get one, by giving money to a charitable cause."

The previous Wednesday, I was at the Lions practice before their Thanksgiving Day game. Down near one end zone I noticed Mike Utley in a wheelchair. As a 290-pound Lions guard, Mike lost his balance during a 1991 game while making a block, stumbled forward, and landed on his head in a freak accident. He suffered a fracture of the sixth cervical vertebra, a broken neck. He was paralyzed from the chest down, but retained the use of his hands and arms. When you see a guy like that in a wheelchair, you always expect him to be down. So when I went over to talk to him, I thought, *I'll try to lift his spirits.*

Instead, he lifted mine.

"Hey, John, I'm doing great," he said. "I'm lifting weights. I'm scuba diving. I'm sky diving."

"You're sky diving?"

"Yeah, it's great," he said. "I need a guy to sky dive with me now, but pretty soon I'll be licensed to go solo."

"How do you land?"

"The first time, I landed face-first, *boom*," he said, laughing, "but it was such a great feeling, I didn't care. After that I learned that if I twist a little, I can land on my side."

"But how can you do that?"

"What am I going to do?" he said, laughing again. "Break my neck?"

When Mike Utley was playing, he was never All-Madden, but he is now.

JOE MONTANA JUST KNEW HOW

The day Joe Montana stood on a platform in Justin Herman Plaza in San Francisco and announced his retirement to the twenty thousand people gathered there, I was asked, "Of all Joe's great games, which one do you remember best?"

"Only one?" I said. "I can pick only one?"

I could've picked a dozen, maybe more, starting with the 49ers' 20–16 win over the Bengals in Super Bowl XXIII when Joe hit John Taylor for a 10-yard touchdown with thirty-four seconds left. Or the 1981 NFC championship game against the Cowboys when his 6-yard pass to Dwight Clark with fifty-one seconds left put the 49ers into Super Bowl XVI. Or his five touchdown passes in the 55–10 rout of the Broncos in Super Bowl XXIV. Or anytime the 49ers were behind in the fourth quarter. The more pressure, the better he was. When he was behind, he always knew he was going to beat you. His teammates knew. The fans knew. And when he really had you was when the other team knew. But as great as he was in all those games for the 49ers, I picked another game.

"His game for the Chiefs against the 49ers," I said.

Joe had been traded to the Chiefs in 1993 but they lost the AFC championship game in Buffalo after he suffered a concussion. When the 1994 season began, it was probably his last time around. The second weekend, the Chiefs were playing the 49ers in Kansas City, the old gunslinger against his old teammates. He had the inferior team, but he was just about perfect. He hit nineteen of thirty-one passes for 206 yards and two touchdowns with no interceptions as the Chiefs won, 24–17, over the 49ers team that would go on to win Super Bowl XXIX.

Joe was thirty-eight then, but he looked like the Joe Montana of seven, eight, ten years earlier. The way he played he made me think of Clemson coach Frank Thomas's line about Alabama coach Paul "Bear" Bryant that Bum Phillips used to describe Don Shula: "He can take his'n and beat your'n, or he can take your'n and beat his'n." For years Joe had taken the 49ers and beat everybody else. Now he had taken the Chiefs and beaten the 49ers. Put him on either team that day, and that team wins.

For all of Joe's genuine greatness as the best offensive player I've seen in my years in the television booth, I also thought he just knew more about offensive football than any other player of his era. Nobody ever talked about that. If his coaches knew it, they didn't mention it, at least not to me. But he enjoyed the chess game, knowing what his team had to do and what the other team was going to try to do, and whenever I was around him, he wasn't afraid to share it.

"The offensive coordinator can call all the plays," he would say, "but as the quarterback, I've got to see the receivers, throw it to 'em and get it to 'em. And with Jerry Rice, get it to him as early in the game as possible."

The longer a quarterback takes to get the ball to his best wide receiver, the more that receiver starts pressing and the more the quarterback starts pressing. Then there's no flow. So a smart quarterback gets his best wide receiver in the flow early. You'll see some games where the star receiver seems to disappear. The other team bumps him, doubles him, gives him all the coverage. But one way or another, Joe would get the ball to Jerry Rice as early in the game as possible.

Every quarterback goes through what coaches call reads and progressions, meaning the read of the defensive pass coverages and the progressions in seeing which pass receiver is open.

Joe did this better than anybody. As he called signals, he read the defense. At the snap, he read it again to see if the defense had changed. Dropping back to pass, he read it again. During that final read, he was also going through his progression of pass receivers. It's a combination of seeing the defense, seeing where his receivers are, then throwing the ball to the right guy at the right time in the right place. All this while avoiding pass rushers.

To Joe, the passing game was like layers. He always had a short receiver up to 5 yards downfield, then a medium receiver from 5 to 10 yards downfield, then a deeper receiver farther down, but all of them were on the same side. That makes it easier for him to read his receivers one-two-three, rather than having to look from one side of the field to the other side.

If his first read wasn't there, Joe went to his second; and if that wasn't there, he went to his third. The time it took you to read that sentence, that's about all the time any quarterback usually has. So your first read is, if the linebacker drops deep, you hit the running back on a short route. If the linebacker stays with that back, you hit the medium receiver behind him. If that medium guy isn't open, you still have time to go to the deep guy coming across. But it's all got to happen simultaneously. If the quarterback takes a three-step drop or a five-step drop while the receiver is running a deeper pattern designed for a seven-step drop, the receiver won't be open. Conversely, if the pass receiver is running a short pattern, say a quick slant, designed for a three-step drop while the quarterback is taking a five-step drop or a seven-step drop, the receiver won't be open either. And even if you're Joe Montana, sometimes the other team comes up with a new defense.

"The last time we played New Orleans," I remember him once telling me, "they took away my tight end and my running back. Now everyone is doing that."

Other teams always tried to take away Jerry Rice, but the 49ers wouldn't let that happen. They used Rice out of the slot or put him in motion or sometimes even lined him up in the backfield, anything to help spring him loose. If he's in the slot or in motion or in the backfield, he's off the line, and the defense isn't allowed to bump him.

Joe understood all that because he knew how to play the game. Not every quarterback does. Some can throw the ball a mile, but they don't really know what they're doing. They waste time-outs. They have third and seven, but they'll throw a 5-yard pass; then their team has to punt. I've never understood that. Sometimes it's third and twenty, and they dump it off to try to get some yards before they punt; I can understand that. But when you're trying to keep a drive going and you need 7 yards, I never can understand why they have a guy run a 2-yard or 3-yard pattern.

Joe Montana didn't make those mistakes. Just like good golfers know how to score even when they're not hitting the ball well, he knew how to score even when his passes weren't clicking on all cylinders.

He knew how to slow down the pace, how to quicken the pace. If he was trying to kill the clock to preserve a lead, he stayed in the huddle longer, he took his time going up to the line of scrimmage, he'd let the play clock get down to two seconds. Conversely, if he needed to save time, he'd go to a quick huddle, in and out; get up to the line; and go on one. You'd think every quarterback would know how to do that, how to slow it down or speed it up; but it doesn't come naturally to everyone.

I think Joe would've been a great quarterback wherever he played. He was one of four quarterbacks on the NFL's seventy-fifth anniversary all-time team with Sammy Baugh, Otto Graham, and Johnny Unitas. But for Joe, I think the difference between just being a great quarterback and being one of the best that ever played was probably the difference between going to another team and going to the 49ers.

Not every good quarterback gets to play with a good team. Archie Manning never did. He was mired down there in New Orleans when the Saints had all those bad years, then he finished up with Minnesota and Houston when neither team was very good. Nobody ever knew how good Archie might have been with a good team. Had something like that happened to Joe, I don't know if he would've been as great. The wear and tear comes earlier, the injuries. He would've had a totally different career.

Not many people know that when Joe Montana came out of Notre Dame in the 1979 draft, Bill Walsh was looking to draft another quarterback that nobody had heard of then: Phil Simms from Morehead State. When the Giants jumped on Simms in the first round, Bill looked around for another quarterback and took Joe Montana, in the third round.

Phil Simms turned out to be a real warrior for the Giants, but he had a tough row to hoe. He had to play in Giants Stadium with that wind blowing all the time and the cold weather late in the season. Even when the Giants won two Super Bowls, they were more dominant on defense than on offense. Phil never had what you would call a really good offensive team around him. He never had great receivers. He always had a pretty good running game, but he didn't always have real good pass protection from his offensive line, especially early in his career when he kept getting hurt.

But when Joe Montana went in the third round, it wasn't that surprising. He didn't have good numbers. He wasn't real big. He wasn't real strong. He wasn't real fast. He was tall enough at six three; but when he was a rookie, he was skinny. I mean, skinny. The 49ers listed him at 200 pounds that year, but I can't believe he weighed more than 185. His last season, the Chiefs listed him at 205, but maybe they counted his shoulder pads. I don't think he ever lifted a weight. The thing was, Joe could play football. He was a quarterback, not just another guy who's on the roster as a quarterback.

Troy Aikman knows how to play football too. With the Cowboys, like the 49ers, everything is rhythm and timing. He takes that quick three-step drop or that five-step drop and lets the ball go. One-two-three, throw. One-two-three-four-five, throw.

Troy is so accurate with his passes because he holds the ball up high. When he throws, it's all torque motion, real short and real quick. That style evolved from the way Don Coryell coached the Chargers when Dan Fouts was their quarterback. One of Don's assistants was Ernie Zampese, who went to the Rams as offensive coordinator in 1983 under John Robinson, who hired Norv Turner as his receivers coach the next year. Norv moved to the Cowboys as Jimmy Johnson's offensive coordinator in 1991, and when Norv was hired as the Redskins' head coach in 1994, Ernie took over as the Cowboys' offensive coordinator. That's why Troy Aikman never missed a beat.

"Norv Turner taught me how to be a quarterback," Troy told me, "and Ernie Zampese won't let me forget how to be one."

Troy appreciates his coaches. Another time I mentioned to him that while there are thirty teams in the NFL now, there aren't thirty quarterbacks that know how to play the game.

"That's true," he said, "but I'll tell you what's even more true. As few quarterbacks as there are, there are fewer good quarterback coaches."

Troy is also as tough as they come. He's had several concussions that he won't talk about. He's got a bad back. He's had shoulder problems, knee problems, leg muscle problems. He wears a knee brace and high-top shoes. He wears a long face mask and a padded chin strap. But he keeps playing.

"We have only sixteen games," he told me. "You can't afford to miss any of 'em."

Brett Favre has that same attitude. Just go play. Two months before his last season at Southern Mississippi, he was in a car that hit a tree and flipped over three times. His stomach muscle wall was ripped open. He lost thirty inches of intestines.

"I've got no feeling on my right side," he told me. "There's no muscle there. They put a piece of plastic in there. You can hear it move around. Listen."

When he rubbed his side, I heard it. But a month after his surgery, he was playing quarterback for Southern Mississippi, leading it to an 8–3 record that was within eight points of an undefeated season. His Packer teammates know how important he is to their Super Bowl chances. Reggie White has said, "We can go a long way with this guy," meaning the quarterback out of Kiln, Mississippi, who was nicknamed "Country Time" by Deion Sanders when they were both on the Falcons before the Packers got him in a trade. Whether it was a football or a baseball, Brett could always throw.

"When I was twelve," he told me, "I was playing right field on a team with guys who were eighteen. If the ball came to me, I just threw it in as hard as I could. Threw it clear over the backstop once."

Now that great arm lets Brett throw the most important pass in pro football, the pass from one hashmark to the other sideline. That might only be a 15-yard gain on the field, but it's a 40-yard pass in the air. If a quarterback can't zing that pass known as an "out," the defense doesn't have to zone that side of the field. That great arm also lets him throw a pass on the run better than anybody. He can roll out, get his shoulders square and wing it, sometimes even when his shoulders aren't square. He made some great strides in 1995 in adjusting to the absence of Sterling Sharpe, his All-Pro wide receiver who suffered a serious neck injury.

"Sterling was great," Brett told me, "but if you didn't get him the ball in the first quarter, he'd sit on the bench with a towel over his head. Now I can move the ball around to more receivers."

That great arm also creates problems. Brett throws some balls he shouldn't throw. Not because he's forcing the pass or because he doesn't know any better but because he has so much confidence in his arm, he thinks he'll drill the ball in there despite all those defensive backs. With some young quarterbacks, interceptions happen because of a lack of confidence but with Brett, his interceptions usually come from too much confidence. Kerry Collins is the same way. He knows he can drill it; and at six five, he doesn't lose sight of his receivers, which many quarterbacks do. But his rookie year with Carolina, he had nineteen interceptions.

Another thing about playing quarterback in the NFL that most people don't know is how much faster things are happening out there on the field than they did in college.

It didn't take long for Steve McNair to realize that. He had thrown for more than 14,000 yards at Alcorn State and when the Oilers finally put him in as a rookie in the second half against the Lions late in the 1995 season, he completed sixteen of twenty-seven passes for 203 yards for one touchdown with one interception. But he felt like he was out there in the middle of an interstate with cars and trucks whizzing by.

"The speed of the pro game," he said later. "People talk about it, but until you're on the field in that pocket you have no idea what they are talking about."

Kerry Collins and Steve McNair are learning how to play the game just like John Elway and Dan Marino and every other good quarterback had to learn how to play.

You watch Elway now, it's like he could take any other ten guys and go out and play and the Broncos would win. He's never had a good running back or a good line, but he knows how to play the game. Marino's the same way. I've always thought that the best pure passer I ever saw was Joe Namath, but for just throwing the ball, Marino is now the closest guy to him. Just watching Dan throw the ball on film—I know it's videotape, but I still call it film—I get mesmerized. He's had some good receivers on the Dolphins, but they've never had a good enough defense. Neither has Drew Bledsoe, who I think is going to be the next great quarterback. Before the Patriots got into the 1994 playoffs, I called Bill Parcells to wish him well and he barked at me like he always does.

"We're not that good," he said. "We don't have any defense."

"But you've got that Bledsoe kid," I said. "If I had him, I'd have him go back and chuck it every play. I'd throw it every down."

"Who am I talking to? Is this John Madden? You can't be the same John Madden I know. You never went back and threw it every down."

"I never had Bledsoe."

But when a quarterback like Aikman or Elway or Marino or Bledsoe is hurt, a coach has to do the best he can with his backup. Sometimes he has to change his system to accommodate the backup, even for as good a quarterback as Steve Young. When Joe Montana missed virtually all of the 1991 and 1992 seasons with an elbow injury and then was traded to the Chiefs, the 49ers' system had to be changed.

That system had been designed around Joe, who is right-handed and did most of his stuff to the right. Steve is left-handed and did most of his stuff to the left. Joe had a quicker release on his passes, but Steve was a much better runner.

All that had to be incorporated into a new system, but the 49ers still had to get the ball to Jerry Rice and John Taylor. If they didn't, they wouldn't be the 49ers. So the system had to be adapted to Steve Young, but he still had to be able to pass the ball and he had to pass it to those two wide receivers. As much as anything else, Steve had to learn to let himself go, to let himself be himself. He's really a nice guy, but as a quarterback you can't always be a nice guy. He has a twice-a-week radio show on KNBR in San Francisco just before mine. When he stayed on the air with me one morning I mentioned that when he was in grammar school, he must've been one of those kids who got an A in deportment. He pretended he didn't know what deportment meant.

"I wasn't very good in geography," he said.

Here's a guy who's a lawyer, so he knew what deportment meant, but he's just a good guy. It's his nature to keep things inside, to respect everybody. Especially when he's at fault. Harris Barton, his 49ers roommate, told me about the time he drove down to Pebble Beach to be in Steve's gallery at the AT&T National Pro-Am golf tournament. Pro football players don't even think about the seventy thousand people in the stadium, but put them on the first tee in a golf tournament with a gallery and they're terrified. Steve just wanted to hit a decent drive and go play golf. But to add to his nervousness, in the AT&T you're introduced.

"From the San Francisco 49ers," the voice on the first tee announced, "quarterback Steve Young."

He walked over, leaned down, teed his ball, stepped back, took a practice swing, and was just about to get into his stance when another voice broke the silence.

"Mr. Young," an official said, "you've got fifteen clubs in your bag."

You're only allowed fourteen clubs. Any other golfer would have walked over and decided which club to take out of his bag. But when Steve heard that, instead of saying anything back, he handed his driver to Harris Barton and said, "Here, hold it for me." Then he grabbed his 3-wood and teed off. Now, with his driver no longer among the clubs in his bag, he couldn't use his driver the rest of the round.

Steve not saying anything to the official, just handing his driver to Harris and saying, "Here, hold it for me," that was typical. He wanted an A in deportment.

When we needed Steve to do an interview for our 1994 All-Madden show after a 49ers practice, he hurried there still wearing his cleats. He wanted another A in deportment.

As the backup to Joe, he was the same way. He didn't want to say anything that would make it look like he wasn't being a good soldier. I don't mean to get psychological here, but in doing that, he held everything within himself, which didn't let him flow as a player. After Joe was hurt and the 49ers were now his team, he started to be himself but he didn't really let himself go until early in the 1994 season when the 49ers were on their way to being blown out, 40–8, by the Eagles at Candlestick Park. He was in the huddle when he felt a tap on his shoulder. George Seifert, not wanting to risk having Steve get hurt in a game that was lost, had sent his backup, Elvis Grbac, to replace him. Steve ran to the sideline and went berserk. He yelled at George and any other coach that tried to talk to him. He yelled at any other player that tried to calm him down.

"I didn't care what the score was," he explained later, "I didn't want to come out of the game."

Coaches seldom apologize to a player for anything, but the next day George Seifert apologized to Steve for taking him out. Steve found out that he could express himself angrily and the coach would understand. I think it got him over a hump. I think even more than his yelling at the coach, his teammates looked at him a little differently. I think he looked at himself a little differently too. And it helped him. He learned that he didn't need to get an A in deportment to be respected.

Before the 1994 playoffs began, Steve still had a "Yeah . . . but" on him. You know the line, "Yeah, Steve Young is a great quarterback, he's the NFL's most valuable player in 1992, and 1994, but he still hasn't won a Super Bowl." When he threw six touchdown passes in a 49–26 rout of the Chargers in Super Bowl XXIX, he finally was rid of his last "Yeah . . . but."

After that game, Steve was so happy, he looked like a little kid who finally got the bicycle he always wanted. That's what I like about him. He still plays like a little kid. He's all spirit and emotion. He's supposed to be a passer, but if there's a run open, he runs. If there's a game to play, he wants to play. During the 1995 season he missed five starts with a shoulder injury. When he came back against the Rams, by early in the fourth quarter the 49ers had a 35–13 lead. But when George Seifert took him out, he blew up again.

He knew George was just trying to keep him from getting hurt, but Steve didn't agree. Hey, if the 49ers are still playing, he wants to play. He's not thinking, *I better watch out, I might get hurt.* In a preseason game a few months earlier, his helmet somehow got knocked off as he was scrambling; but he kept running for yardage, and he didn't look to get out of bounds.

Running without your helmet, that's a football player. I'm not saying it's the smartest thing to do. I'm not saying everyone should do it. But if you're running without your helmet in a preseason game, you're competing and you're not worrying about anything. That's why Steve Young is Steve Young, and he did it during a preseason when there was more talk than ever about guys not playing because they might get hurt or coaches not playing guys because they might get hurt. Maybe free agency has something to do with it. Some players don't want to risk blowing that big contract and some coaches don't want to risk losing a high-salaried player. But, as a player or a coach, if you start worrying about getting hurt or your players getting hurt, you can't stay in the game.

Steve's running ability has developed the bootleg pass into the 49ers' most effective play and one of the NFL's most popular plays. The drop-back pass is still the most popular, the second most popular is the play pass where you fake a run, then drop back. The bootleg pass would be third, the roll-out pass fourth.

The bootleg pass is just a variation of the old bootleg run where the quarterback turned his back, faked a hand-off to a running back going one way, and hid the ball on his hip and ran the other way. That was always a good play near the goal line, but the 49ers and other teams now use the bootleg pass all over the field on any down; and with Steve Young such a threat to run, it's even more effective. He's not only the 49ers' best quarterback, he's their best running back. If the other team drops off, he can run. If it comes up on him, he tosses the ball to Jerry Rice or Brent Jones coming across.

During those five games in 1995 when Steve Young was out with a bruised shoulder, I had an idea. If I ever went back to coaching, which I never will, I'd hire a special assistant coach just for the backup quarterbacks.

The way the game is played now, the only quarterback

who practices with the game plan is the starter. He usually gets every snap. The backup and the emergency quarterback get none. During the week before the fourth of the five games Steve missed in 1995, George Seifert was talking like Steve might start against the Carolina Panthers even though everybody else thought the backup, Elvis Grbac, would start. George was probably doing it to keep Carolina guessing but when I talked to Elvis that Saturday at practice, he didn't know what to think.

"I've been taking snaps in practice," he said, "but nobody has told me if I'm starting or not."

The thing that's tough about that, when the quarterbacks meet with the offensive coordinator, everything in the game plan is directed to the starting quarterback. The backup might as well not even be there. The offensive coordinator explains everything to the starter, and if there are any questions, the starter asks them. The backup can't say, "Hey, wait a minute, what happens if I'm in there?" Part of being a backup is deferring to the starter. But the point is, if the backup is going to start, he should be asking his own questions because they're probably not the same questions as the starter's questions.

As it turned out, Elvis did start, Steve didn't play at all, and the 49ers lost to Carolina, an expansion team, 13–7. Maybe the preparation of the quarterbacks was not a factor. Maybe it was.

That's when I thought about how maybe teams should have an assistant coach just for the backup quarterbacks. I know, most teams already have too many assistant coaches. When I was coaching the Raiders, I never had more than seven assistants. When the Cowboys played in Oakland in 1995, they used the old Raiders locker room in the Coliseum so I went down there to look around just for old times' sake. The assistant coaches' locker room still had eight lockers but the Cowboys had thirteen assistants. I don't know how they split up those lockers.

Even so, if I were coaching now, in addition to an offensive coordinator, I'd want an ex-quarterback to coach my quarterbacks, to watch them every play during a game. I'd also want another assistant coach to work with the backup quarterback and the emergency quarterback.

If you're too busy with the starting quarterback to prepare your other quarterbacks, if you don't let them ask questions in the meeting, and if you don't give them snaps in practice, then they're obviously the least important players on your team that week. But if the starter goes down, the backup suddenly goes from being your least important player to your most important. If the backup goes down, the emergency quarterback suddenly is your most important player. And neither has had any special coaching directed at them that week. I know they're supposed to be absorbing the game plan and watching films and imagining themselves being out there, but that's different from doing it.

I'd want my backup-quarterback coach to take the same game plan the starter has, but put it in for the backup and emergency quarterbacks. Answer their questions. Maybe add a few plays that are more suited to them than to the starter.

That's what Bill Parcells did for Jeff Hostetler when the Giants won Super Bowl XXV. Phil Simms had been the starter until he went down with a severely damaged ankle late in the season. I didn't think any backup could take a team through the playoffs and the Super Bowl, but Jeff did. In the NFC championship game in San Francisco, the Giants won, 15–13, on Matt Bahr's five field goals but Hostetler got the job done. Nothing spectacular but solid. No big mistakes. When the Giants beat the Bills, 20–19, in Super Bowl XXV at Tampa the following Sunday, he got the job done again.

I've respected Jeff ever since, especially when I almost caused him to miss the Giants' chartered jet from San Francisco to Tampa.

After the Giants won that NFC championship game, I had to do interviews for a Super Bowl preview right there in Candlestick Park. Bill Parcells and a few Giants players came out. Jeff was the last one and he was hurting. He had an ice pack on his knee. And he could've zinged me for having said on the air that you can't win the NFC championship with your backup quarterback, but he didn't. When we were through, Jeff limped away. But when I got out to where my bus was parked behind the locker rooms, I saw Jeff wandering around. All the Giants' buses to the San Francisco International Airport had left without him.

"Jeff, get on my bus," I said. "We'll get you to the airport."

Except that none of us knew how to get to where the Giants' charter was. To make it worse, we were late. All that Jeff knew was that it was a United Airlines charter so the assistant director on our CBS telecasts then, Richie Zyontz, phoned United.

"We've got the Super Bowl quarterback with us," he said. "We've got to get him to the Giants' charter that's going to Tampa for the Super Bowl."

The voice at United reservations put Richie through to operations. But instead of leaving from a gate in the main terminal, the jet was parked in the cargo area. When we got there, baggage handlers were still loading the Giants' suitcases and equipment trunks. We dropped Jeff off, and he went up the stairs into the jet.

That was the least I could do for a backup quarterback I had said could never win the NFC championship game, much less the Super Bowl.

MY LOCKER ROOM EXCEPTION: EMMITT SMITH

I've always figured I don't belong in a team's locker room after a game. I enjoy talking to players on my bus if they stop by after or before a game, but that's different. It's my bus. But it's their locker room. I just think that's not a place for me to go after a game.

I've made one exception.

When the Cowboys beat the Giants, 16–13, in overtime in their last game of the 1993 season I went into their locker room at Giants Stadium to see Emmitt Smith. He had rushed for 168 yards and caught ten passes for another 61 yards, including a 5-yard touchdown pass. But the big thing was, 78 of those yards came after he suffered a separated right shoulder late in the second quarter. That's one of football's most painful injuries. Most players disappear into the X-ray room and don't play for a few weeks, but Emmitt sucked it up. You could see him wincing but he not only played, he played great.

In overtime he ran or caught a pass nine times for 41 of the 52 yards in the drive that set up the winning field goal in a big game for both teams. The winner finished first in the NFC East and had the home-field advantage throughout the playoffs. The loser was the wild card.

The weather, like it always is late in the season in Giants Stadium, was cold, and the wind made it even colder. But he gained 78 yards when he couldn't lift his right arm. I remember thinking how this has to be one of the great warriors. On my way down in the elevator, I realized I had to make an exception to my rule about not going into a locker room after a game. Inside the door I saw Jimmy Johnson, the Cowboys' coach then.

"Who do you need?" Jimmy asked.

"I just want to congratulate Emmitt on one of the toughest, most courageous games I've seen anyone ever play."

"C'mon into the trainer's room and tell him yourself."

Emmitt was stretched out on the trainer's table, with a bag of ice on his right shoulder. He'd been sedated, he seemed a little out of it but when he looked up, I said, "Congratulations on a great game." He heard me. He smiled, and we shook hands. To this day, I don't know if he remembers me coming in to see him, but that's not important. What's important is what he did in that game with his clavicle and scapula bones torn away from each other. Imagine how painful that is.

You hear people talking about how the players are overpaid. You hear people say, "If I got paid like the players do, I'd play hurt too." But no one who says that would have done what Emmitt Smith did in that game and in the playoffs when his shoulder still hurt.

In the Cowboys' divisional playoff two weeks later against the Packers, he rushed for 60 yards and caught two passes for 27 yards. In the NFC championship game against the 49ers he rushed for 88 yards, caught seven passes for 85 yards, and scored two touchdowns. In Super Bowl XXVIII against the Bills he rushed for 132 yards, caught four passes for 26 yards, and scored two touchdowns. Nobody even counted all the blocks he threw in those three games. All this with a right shoulder that needed surgery a month later to put it back together properly.

That's why Emmitt Smith, to me, is now pro football's best running back and one of its best players.

For just taking the ball and running and you try to catch him and tackle him, Barry Sanders is the best pure runner now. But if you want a running back to do everything a running back has to do, run the ball, catch the ball, and block either in pass protection or for somebody else running the ball, Emmitt Smith is the best. He's not that big. He's listed at five nine and 209, but he plays big. He's like Walter Payton was. Walter was five ten and 202; but for all of his rushing records with the Bears, when I asked Walter once what he got the most satisfaction from, he never hesitated.

"Blocking," he said.

I've never asked Emmitt Smith that question, but he's the same type of running back that Walter was. Whatever the position calls for, they're not only going to do it, they're going to do it better than anyone else. If a running back stays in there on second and third down, he better be a good blocker, especially in pass protection. If a running back can't pass protect, especially on an obvious passing down like third and seven, the defense will take advantage of him by blitzing.

When I watch Emmitt block, either in pass protection or when Daryl Johnston carries the ball, I know that somewhere he had a coach who gave him good fundamentals. Blocking is not only wanting to do it, but also knowing how to do it, like getting underneath the guy you're blocking. Emmitt blocks too well not to have had good fundamentals. When he's pass protecting, he'll put blitzing linebackers on their head.

That's why, if Emmitt isn't playing because he's too hurt to play, the Cowboys just aren't the same team.

I'm sure Emmitt practices his blocking technique, but a running back like Emmitt or Barry Sanders doesn't practice running with the ball. He practices running through the plays, and his coaches remind him of the blocking on those plays, like a guard pulling or a tackle protecting the backside, but he's coached only on what the other guys are doing, not what he has to do. You can't tell a great running back how to run with a football. He does it instinctively. He can't even explain how he does it.

In trying to learn how players think, I've asked Barry Sanders all kinds of questions. What's his first step? What does he see? What makes him cut? He doesn't know. He can't explain why he cuts back the other way. He just does it.

But if you were to ask an average running back about his first step, he might say, "I put my right foot back, then I take a half-step with my left foot," and he'll take you through the whole run. But that run probably wouldn't be for much yardage. It would be too slow, too deliberate, too thought out, too carried out. It would be an action, instead of being a reaction to what happens after he got the ball. You can't get that same reaction in practice. Back when John Riggins was the Redskins' fullback, he wasn't lazy but he hated to practice.

"It never looks the same in a game," John told me. "In a game, everything is so much quicker and you have to react so much quicker. In practice you can get in bad habits. In practice the hole is there and you run through it. But in a game the hole never seems to be where it is in practice. Why practice going through a hole that's not going to be there in the game?"

I've seen a lot of great backs, but when that hole isn't there, I've never seen anybody squirt away for yardage like Barry Sanders does. He's another short guy. He's listed at five nine, although I think he's really five seven or eight;

but notice that I describe him as short, not small. Even if his listed weight (203 pounds) is more than he really weighs, he's not a small guy. He's a short, solid guy. I've always thought that's an advantage for a running back, that height is a disadvantage. When you're short, there's less of you to hit. When you're short, it's easier to get your shoulder closer to your knee. The short guy can bend easier. The short guy doesn't give you anything to hit.

As great as Barry is, until Scott Mitchell set several Lions passing records in 1995, he never had a really good passing game to keep the defense honest. If a quarterback's best friend is a good running game, a running back's best friend is a good passing game.

If you don't pass much, or if the defense doesn't think you can pass, then they're going to bring eight men up on the line to jam the running plays. If you're going against one of Buddy Ryan's teams, he'll bring nine men up, maybe ten. Buddy will dare you to pass. Or if the Lions are playing in Green Bay or Chicago in cold weather late in the season, and they bring eight men up, you can't run against it because there will always be an extra defensive man free.

Some people think that when the Lions didn't have a passing game, Barry was able to run the ball more and that's why he has rushed for so many yards. But if you don't have a passing game, those are the toughest yards you're ever going to get. And he got them.

The thing I could never understand is that until the 1995 season, when the Lions were in short-yardage situations (third down with less than 2 yards to go for a first down) or in goal-line situations (third down inside the 2-yard line), coach Wayne Fontes often took Barry out of the game. Wayne's answer was that as elusive as Barry is, he might lead the NFL in a stat nobody keeps—the number of times he loses yardage looking for a hole.

But on the most important running down you can have, short yardage near the goal line, it never made any sense to me to take out one of the greatest running backs that ever played.

At a quick glance, you wouldn't take Barry Sanders for a football player. He's short and silent. He told me that when he was taking night courses at Oakland (Michigan) Community College during the season a few years ago, none of the other students recognized him.

"If they did," he told me, "they didn't say anything to me."

He preferred it that way. He's a shy guy with a sly sense of humor. When I once asked him where he got all his quick moves from, he looked at me with that deadpan face.

"Mark van Eeghen," he said.

When I was coaching the Raiders, Mark van Eeghen was one of my fullbacks and a good one, but he was a workhorse, not a racehorse. I don't know how Barry knew about Mark van Eeghen, but he knew. Another time I was talking to Barry about his contract. Without thinking, I asked, "How much do you make now?"

With that same deadpan face, he looked up at me and said, "How much do you make now?"

He reminded me that, whatever his contract was for, it was none of my business. Several weeks later a writer was doing a magazine article on me. As we talked, he said, "Let's go over your contract. How much do you get paid?"

"Let's go over your contract," I said. "How much are you getting paid for this article?"

When a running back plays game after game, he takes an awful physical beating. He gets hit from every angle. He won't feel it too much after the game but when he gets out of bed on Monday morning, he'll be stiff and he'll wonder where all those bruises came from. Receivers only get really hit when they catch a pass over the middle. Quarterbacks take some hits but the guys that get hit by more people in more different spots are the running backs.

That's what makes Marcus Allen so remarkable. Going into the 1996 season, he had been taking those hits for fourteen years while rushing for nearly eleven thousand yards as a tailback. It's not unusual for an old quarterback or an old lineman or an old kicker or even an old fullback to play fifteen years, but you don't see too many old tailbacks playing that long. Tailbacks usually get worn down, but Marcus is still fresh and lean. He doesn't even look worn down.

The closer to the goal line, the better Marcus is. He's rushed for 103 touchdowns. He needs only 8 more to break Walter Payton's record of 110. Jim Brown had 106; John Riggins, 104. Getting into that end zone isn't always strength. Sometimes it's feel, vision, patience, knowing where the hole is, and knowing where it isn't.

Touchdowns are the reward for all those bruises a running back gets. To soothe those bruises, more and more running backs are getting massages. Some teams have a masseur who comes in, sets up a table, and works on players all day. Boxers and tennis players have always had massages, but it's new in football. Rodney Hampton, who holds the Giants' career rushing record, swears by the massage.

"I have four or five a week," he told me. "But for me, an hour isn't enough. I need an hour and a half."

Near the end of the season, a workhorse running back won't start feeling well until Thursday, then he'll try to stay fresh for Sunday's game. If he's the least banged up, he hardly practices because the main thing is how fresh he is on Sunday, not how he practices. But even when a workhorse running back is fresh, he has to be constantly reminded to protect the ball against a fumble. When you're running with the ball, you're supposed to hold it in your outside hand, so if you're on the sideline and get hit, the ball will go out of bounds.

For years no matter where Emmitt Smith was, he

always carried the ball in his left hand. He tried to learn to switch it, but he went back to carrying it in his left hand because he wanted his right hand free for balance, especially when you cut. If you put the ball in there tight with both hands, you can't really cut.

When you feel you're about to get hit, you better get that other hand over the ball to protect it because now all the tacklers are doing what Lawrence Taylor brought in, that chop. The tackler comes in from behind, swings one of his arms like a butcher's cleaver, and chops the running back's arm carrying the ball, hoping to cause a fumble. Linemen, linebackers, defensive backs, they all tackle that way now. This really creates a dilemma for a coach, because when you're talking to a running back you never use the word *fumble*. You never tell him, "Don't fumble." Saying that to a running back is like telling a golfer, "Don't shank." In golf you never use the word *shank* and in football you never use the word *fumble*.

What you tell a running back is, "Protect the ball at all times." You try to talk in a positive way, not a negative way.

Back when Vince Lombardi was coaching the Packers, if he had a rookie running back who kept fumbling in training camp, that rookie would have to carry a football around wherever he went. Carry it to lunch. Carry it to dinner. Carry it to his room in the dorm at St. Norbert's College near Green Bay where the Packers trained. Carry it to breakfast the next morning. Carry it back to practice. Carry it just about everywhere until he stopped fumbling. But if he kept fumbling, he didn't have to carry that football around anymore. He'd be cut.

Good running backs seldom fumble. If they happen to, they usually make up for it with a big play, like Ricky Watters seemed to do whenever he fumbled after joining the Eagles in 1995 as a free agent.

Just as Emmitt Smith does it all and excels as a runner, Ricky Watters does it all and excels as a pass receiver. For a running back, Ricky is probably the best receiver I've ever seen. He's such a good receiver; until he joined the Eagles, his coaches at the 49ers and before that at Notre Dame always wanted him catching passes. The 49ers liked to line him up in the backfield, then put him in motion to get him out there as a receiver. Sometimes they lined him up in the slot or as a wide receiver. His last season with the 49ers he caught sixty-six passes for 719 yards and he rushed 239 times for 877 yards. That adds up to 1,596 yards. But for Ricky, the 305 times he handled the ball that season weren't enough.

"I want to be 'The Man,'" he said after joining the Eagles. "I want the ball."

Ricky not only wanted the ball, he demanded the ball. During the late-season game with the Cowboys, he didn't think he was getting the ball often enough, so he talked to the Eagles' offensive coordinator, Jon Gruden. During the first half, he had rushed only nine times for 30 yards. In the second half, he had twenty-four carries for 82 yards, including a 1-yard touchdown, for a total of thirty-three carries for 112 yards in the Eagles' 20–17 win. His impatience with not getting the ball reflected the impatience that Walter Payton had noticed in the way Ricky ran with the 49ers. Before he went to training camp with the Eagles, he happened to be talking to Walter.

"He suggested that I be more patient," Ricky told me. "He thought I hit the hole too hard, that I didn't let stuff develop. He didn't mean run in there soft, but let it develop, then hit it."

Ricky will probably always be a little impatient. He's a fiery emotional guy. That's the way he is. That's why Ray Rhodes wanted him. Before taking over as the Eagles' coach in 1995, Ray had been the 49ers' defensive coordinator when Ricky was there. Ray knew if Ricky didn't get the ball, he would pout; but Ray also knew that if Ricky did get the ball, he could be "The Man." He was. In his first season with the Eagles, he got the ball 399 times, rushing 337 times for 1,273 yards and catching sixty-two passes for 434 yards.

When a defensive coordinator is trying to put a game plan together, he tries to figure out which offensive players he hopes to take away from the other team and in which order. The toughest guy to defend, the second toughest, the third toughest. That's an old George Allen principle. To stop the other team, which of their offensive weapons do you try to take away?

With the 49ers' passing game, you had to try first to take away Jerry Rice if you could; but when the 49ers won Super Bowl XXIX, to me Ricky Watters was the second toughest 49ers weapon. Tight end Brent Jones was the third toughest, and wide receiver John Taylor the fourth toughest. When other defensive coordinators have to put together a game plan now against the Eagles, the toughest guy to defend is Ricky Watters. He gave the Eagles what he had given the 49ers, a third wide receiver without having to substitute.

Whenever a third wide receiver comes in, the other team will put in a fifth defensive back, its nickel defense. But when Ricky Watters comes out of the huddle and lines up as a wide receiver, it's too late for the nickel.

Back when Bill Walsh was the 49ers' head coach, Roger Craig was his receiver coming out of the backfield or out of the slot. Bill never had a great runner. He couldn't establish the running game like most coaches always tried to, so early in the game he would pass all the time. In the second half, when the other team thought he was going to keep passing, his running backs would get yards because by then the defense would be loosened up and spread out. The old theory had been, run early. When you get the other team's defense up on the line to stop the run, then you throw the ball. Bill did the opposite. He came out passing to loosen 'em up and spread 'em out. His running backs liked that. For them, the toughest yards are always early in the game when the other team's defense is fresh and quick. By the fourth quarter, those big linemen and linebackers would all lose a step or two while you hope you haven't.

Any running back who can line up as a wide receiver, like Ricky Watters, is a much more dangerous weapon than the third-down back who comes in when it's third and long. Because as soon as that third-down back trots onto the field, the other team puts its nickel defense on the field.

Even so, one of those third-down backs, David Meggett, not only has been a weapon for the Giants and the Patriots, his name defines what he does: third-down back, punt returner, and kickoff returner. But when he joined the Giants as a fifth-round draft choice out of Towson State (in Maryland) in 1989, Bill Parcells didn't even want him. Meggett was only five seven and 180, and Bill's primary running back then, Joe Morris, wasn't much bigger at five seven and 195.

"What am I going to do with this kid?" Bill asked the Giants' scouts.

"Pitch it to him," one scout suggested. "Run him on a reverse."

"What do you guys think this is?" Bill barked. "The Blue–Gray game?"

Somehow the scouts talked Bill into taking him. Meggett developed into such a versatile and valuable player, he had such an impact on the NFL that every team wanted "a Meggett," somebody who could catch passes, run the ball, and return punts and kickoffs. As good as the Giants were in his years there, Meggett was their only speed player who could make the defense worry, who could beat you with one play, sometimes even a touchdown pass off the option. He and Phil Simms had what they called a "scat" play. Simms would drop back, Meggett would go through the line, then go anywhere he thought he could get open, inside or outside, and Simms would find him with a pass. I once asked Simms how he knew where Meggett would be when Meggett didn't know where he would be.

"After you've done it enough, you learn to look at the same things he's looking at," Phil told me. "If you know what he's looking at and they're the same things you're looking at, then you know what he sees and you know what he's going to do when he sees that."

Meggett was such a good weapon, when he became a free agent after the 1994 season, Parcells, now the Patriots' coach, who hadn't wanted him in 1989, signed him to a five-year ten-million-dollar contract. Joe Gibbs had to laugh when he read that. Back when Joe Gibbs was the Redskins' coach and Bobby Beathard was their general manager, they liked and respected each other, but they would jab each other's draft choices. When Meggett turned out to be such a good player for the Giants, Joe really got on Bobby.

"One of Bobby's sons went to Towson State," Joe told me. "We signed every prospect from Towson State except the two who could really play, Meggett and Landeta."

Sean Landeta, who the Giants signed in 1985 after the U.S. Football League folded, was chosen as the punter on the NFL's All-Eighties team. But as good as David Meggett is, as soon as he came in on third down, the other team would blitz. Not that he couldn't pass block, but if he were in there to be a pass receiver, the blitz would make him stay in the backfield to block. That's the difference between a third-down back and an every-down back like Emmitt Smith. There's really no defense for somebody like Emmitt Smith, sometimes not even when he has a shoulder separation.

JERRY RICE IS THE BEST

One day at the 49ers' complex, I stopped by Jerry Rice's locker and joked about how he always looks so good in his uniform.

"I've always believed that if you look bad in your uniform, you play good," I said. "And if you look good, you play bad."

Jerry is the exception that proves my rule. He really believes that he has to look good. He spends a lot of time primping not just for games, but for practices. He makes sure everything about his 49ers uniform fits perfectly. His jersey is tucked in. His little hand towel is hanging just so. He has his new gloves with *JR* on them for each game. His white socks are brand-new. His football shoes have to be so clean, they look brand-new.

"If you don't look good," he told me, "you can't play good."

I always smile at that, but to him it's not funny. We don't argue about it; but when he talks about it, he's serious. He's not laughing. That's because he's a perfectionist. Even when I go to a 49ers practice, I can't help but watch him. Whatever the play, he goes full speed. And with Jerry Rice, full speed is his speed. If it's a pass to him, he catches the ball, runs full speed downfield, then runs back to the huddle. If it's a pass to another receiver or a running play, he runs his assignment full speed, then runs back to the huddle.

Not just most plays. Every play.

That work ethic is what makes Jerry Rice so special. He's not only better than any of the other wide receivers, he works harder than any of the others. You don't see that combination too often: where the guy that's the best also works the hardest. Usually the overachiever is the hardest worker, a little guy who runs hard in practice to impress the coaches, who stays after practice hoping the coaches will notice.

Jerry Rice does all those things even though he's the best. And that's why he is the best.

With defensive backs changing on almost every down and with the shorter play clock, wide receivers need the stamina of an Olympic distance runner. In order to go hard almost every play, they need to train hard almost every day. Even in the off-season. Jerry Rice has been known to start his workouts at seven o'clock; he does various stretching exercises and warmup sprints for thirty minutes, runs two or three hills that are anywhere from a mile to two miles long for another thirty minutes, runs ten to fourteen sprints of about one hundred yards on a football field, does pass-catching drills for another thirty minutes, lifts weights for two and a half hours, and finishes up with a StairMaster workout for another thirty to forty-five minutes. That's a workout of nearly five hours, in the off-season.

But that's Jerry Rice. Everything he does is thought out. How he trains. How he practices. How he looks in his uniform. Even how he warms up before a game.

Steve Young is the 49ers' only left-handed quarterback, which means the spin on his passes is just the opposite from those of a right-handed quarterback. With a left-handed quarterback, the ball rotates to the left; with a right-handed quarterback it rotates to the right. But on Saturday, a team's starting quarterback seldom throws in practice. So when the 49ers are practicing on Saturday, you'll see Jerry catching passes from their left-handed equipment man, Ted Walsh, just to stay in sync with the spin on Steve Young's passes. He also warms up with Ted on the sideline before a game.

Now you know how Jerry Rice made himself into the best wide receiver that ever played.

But when he arrived as a rookie, the 49ers' first-round choice in 1985 out of little Mississippi Valley State, he wasn't the best who ever played. I mean, he made himself into the best who ever played. Then when Joe Montana left, he made himself adjust to Steve Young's passes, not just the spin but also the timing. All those years he and Montana were in such good sync, he was catching the ball on the run without breaking stride, especially on that little slant over the middle. Montana would take that three-step drop, Rice would pop open, and Montana would hit him in stride in the seam between the linebacker and the defensive back; then he would run right through the defense.

But when Montana was hurt in 1991 and Young took over, Rice wasn't in sync with Young right away. Especially on that slant.

Montana would take that three-step drop, and Rice would be open coming across from the right side. But when Young went one-two-three, because he was left-handed, he had to turn more to the right than Montana did. That split-second difference threw off the timing. The ball was released half a beat late, so the ball got to Rice half a beat late. He'd have to reach back to catch it. Or he'd catch it and get tackled. Or he'd miss it and take a hit. That half a beat made a difference.

So the 49ers lined up Rice on the left side more often,

which let Young go one-two-three, *boom*, just pop it in there to Rice coming across from the left side the same way Montana did when Rice was coming across from the right side. By now they've played together enough that they can hit that slant pass with Rice coming from the right side.

No matter what the other team does, Jerry Rice can beat it. If you start coming up on the slant, he goes deep. If you think you're about to tackle him, he's so strong, he'll break the tackle or make you miss. In the 49ers' offense that Bill Walsh devised, he became the prototype. The tall wide receiver that's a big target, that can run the slant, that can run after the catch. Some receivers catch a 12-yard pass, and they fall down for a 12-yard gain. If Jerry catches a 12-yard pass he might turn it into a 52-yard touchdown. He doesn't have blazing speed, but he has the hands, the concentration, the toughness, the strength.

That's why, going into the 1996 season, he held three career NFL records with 942 receptions for 15,123 yards and 156 touchdowns.

There's another reason why he's the best. He's a complete receiver. He's a good blocker. He'll make big blocks downfield to spring a teammate. When you see a wide receiver blocking, it's 99 percent hustle. He doesn't have to be devastating. He doesn't have to level tacklers. He just has to get downfield and get in the way. Not every wide receiver does it. Jerry Rice does it.

He's always been tough. Teams tried to intimidate him. Punch him. Rough him up. If anything bothered him, it was getting bumped at the line of scrimmage. Not that he was bothered physically, but it threw off his timing with Joe Montana or Steve Young.

If I were still coaching, the first thing I'd do is double Jerry Rice, then I'd tell my defensive backs to leave him alone. Don't say a word to him. Pat him on the back. Don't get him fired up. Don't make him any tougher to stop than he already is.

The best wide receivers are always tougher than they look. Jerry Rice's teammate John Taylor not only caught touchdown passes—like the 10-yard dart from Joe Montana with thirty-four seconds remaining in Super Bowl XXIII that beat the Bengals 20–16—he also ran back punts, until he got a bad knee. He was a good blocker, and he could run with the ball after he caught it.

Michael Irvin is another tough guy. Jimmy Johnson realized that when he had Michael at the University of Miami in 1984, long before he was the Cowboys' coach.

"I heard about this fight in the cafeteria between Michael and a big lineman," Jimmy once told me. "Michael was just a skinny freshman, the lineman was a senior. I assumed Michael had gotten the worst of it, but then I found out Michael decked him. The lineman had tried to cut in front of Michael on the food line."

Big mistake. When you grow up in Fort Lauderdale, Florida, in a poor family of seventeen kids, you don't let anyone mess with your food.

"I didn't know much about Michael at the time," Jimmy told me, "but when he decked the lineman, I knew I had a football player."

So when Michael Irvin goes up to catch a pass that he thinks is his, it's not that much different from his going up against that big lineman who was trying to cut in front of him in the cafeteria. That toughness he showed in the cafeteria that day is the same toughness that makes him want the ball as the NFL's most physical wide receiver. Even against double-coverage, he's out there where the quarterback can find him. Sometimes he's accused of pushing off to get open, but he gets open. It doesn't take a big push because all you're doing is redirecting the defensive back and separating yourself from him. If you get a hand below the waist, the officials don't always see it, but if you get it up high, they usually do. And the Cowboys throw the ball to him more often than they do to anybody else. Back when Norv Turner was the Cowboys' offensive coordinator, he once stopped and looked at me while talking about the X's and O's in their game plan.

"I don't know why I'm being so technical," Norv said. "All we have to do is give the ball to Emmitt Smith and throw the ball to Michael."

When the Cowboys had Alvin Harper—a real leaper who high-jumped seven feet one inch in high school in Frostproof, Florida—they threw the ball to him, too. He could catch a pass at its highest point. The Cowboys knew that better than anyone, no matter who their quarterback was. When they were getting ready to play the Packers in their 1994 Thanksgiving Day game, Troy Aikman was hurt. Jason Garrett, the backup who had hardly played, would be starting.

"My wife told me what to do," I remember Jason saying. "Just throw the ball high to Alvin."

That's what Jason did. He completed fifteen of twenty-six passes for 311 yards and two touchdowns, including three to Alvin for 91 yards and a touchdown in a 42–31 win. But the Cowboys didn't throw the ball to Alvin often enough, at least not for him.

He joined the Tampa Bay Buccaneers as a free agent. He got a big contract. He had developed into a feared second guy alongside Michael Irvin. If you left Alvin alone, he could beat you. In the 1992 NFC championship game in San Francisco he set up two touchdowns with three receptions for 117 yards in the Cowboys' 30–20 win. But in going to Tampa Bay, he all but disappeared. When a player goes to some teams, it's like he's never seen again. At least not on national television. Teams like Tampa Bay, Arizona, Seattle, Cincinnati, the Jets, they hardly ever play in the late Sunday afternoon national game, the Sunday night game, or the Monday night game. Out of sight, out of mind.

Some guys can't miss no matter what team they're with, but others need to be in the right place, the right system, like tight ends Jay Novacek and Brent Jones.

When the Cowboys signed Jay Novacek in 1990, he was what was known then as a Plan B free agent the Arizona Cardinals had not protected. The 49ers signed Brent Jones after the Steelers waived him early in the 1986 season. Neither one is a devastating blocker, but they give you other things.

Jay Novacek's value to the Cowboys is the value Troy Aikman puts on him. Troy is real comfortable with him.

"I don't want to play quarterback anymore," Troy has often said, "if Jay Novacek is not my tight end."

Every quarterback has to have a receiver that, no matter what happens, he'll get the quarterback off the hook. Novacek is Aikman's guy. When the Cowboy coaches are putting together their game plan every week, they know that this play or that play will almost always work because Aikman and Novacek will almost always make it work.

The best tight end I ever had with the Raiders was Dave Casper. When you needed a block, he could block like a lineman. When you needed a receiver, he could catch passes like a wide receiver.

With some tight ends, if they are good blockers, you never throw them the ball and if they are good receivers, you never ask them to block. But you could do both with Dave Casper, just like the Giants did both with Mark Bavaro on their Super Bowl teams. If you had to throw the ball, Bavaro was a threat on that seam pass from Phil Simms up the middle. If you needed him to block, he was a good blocker.

Brent Jones is not as complete a tight end as Casper and Bavaro were, but he's perfect for the 49ers' system. He'll block, although he's a much better pass receiver. But at six four and 230 pounds, he's big enough that the other team can't say he's not a blocker. He's fast enough that the 49ers occasionally line him up all the way to the sideline like a wide receiver, with Jerry Rice moving into the slot.

The Cowboys do the same thing with Novacek, lining him up wide with Michael Irvin in the slot.

Rice and Irvin really benefit from that. When a wide receiver is on the line of scrimmage, a defensive back can get up close and bump him right away. If he's in the slot, between another wide receiver and a tackle or a tight end, he's a yard back from the line of scrimmage. Now the defensive back can't get that close to him. Plus if you're in the slot, you can go in motion and that makes it that much harder for a defensive back to bump you. That little edge is all Rice and Irvin ever ask. But it goes back to their tight ends being good enough and fast enough to line up as wide receivers. When your tight end is more of a weapon than your third or fourth wide receiver, you don't have to take him out. Just line him up as a wide receiver.

Another reason why the Cowboys and the 49ers have been dominating the Super Bowls.

MY FAVORITE BIG OL' GUYS

Nate Newton was flat on his back. His 323 pounds, his listed weight as a Cowboys guard the last time I looked, weren't moving. His teammates were staring down at him. I'm hoping he's all right. He's one of my favorite guys. But up in the booth, as I stared at the tight shot of him on my monitor, I noticed a torn Snickers candy bar wrapper near him.

I'd never seen a candy bar wrapper on a football field, but before I could talk about that, I had to make sure that big ol' Nate was all right. I didn't want to be talking about a candy bar wrapper if he were seriously injured. But as soon as Nate moved around and got up, one of our cameramen zoomed in on the Snickers wrapper.

"Someone got a candy bar knocked out of him," I said. "Someone had a candy bar on his person."

But when Nate heard about what I said about the candy bar wrapper, he didn't think it was funny. The next time I saw him, he jumped on me about it.

"You were trying to say I pack candy bars when I play," he said. "That I keep candy bars in my uniform and one fell out."

"I just said you need candy bars for fuel," I told him. "You got hit so hard, it knocked the wrapper off one of 'em."

I wouldn't have done that with too many players, but I thought I could do it with Nate Newton because he's always joking about his size and how much he can eat. In the off-season he's been close to four hundred pounds. But he didn't appreciate me talking about the candy bar wrapper.

"I had people ask me, 'Do you keep candy bars in your pants?'" he said. "My grandmother even called me to ask."

The more we talked, the more Nate started laughing about it. He's just a good guy. He enjoys life, enjoys football. He has an opinion on everything. If you want to talk about what's happening in the world, what's happening in politics, what's happening anywhere, Nate's your man. And there's another reason I like him. Some players never give much credit to any of their teammates. Nate always does.

"I was just an average overweight journeyman guard until Emmitt Smith came here, then I became a Pro Bowl player," he once told me. "I'm the same guy, but blocking for Emmitt, all you have to do is give him a little crack of daylight."

Nate told me that Emmitt doesn't want any of his offensive linemen talking to him about their blocking, that Emmitt's theory is, "Don't tell me what you're going to do, just go do it. If you tell me, it takes the instinct away from me." Nate always reminds the other Cowboy linemen not to talk to Emmitt during the game, not to say "I can get my guy" or "My guy's taking the inside" or "You can cut back on my guy." Emmitt doesn't want to hear any of that.

"Emmitt's thing," Nate told me, "is, 'I don't react with my ears, I react with my eyes. I don't care what you tell me, I've got to see it. When I see it, then I react.'"

But whenever Emmitt Smith or any running back sees that little crack of daylight, his offensive linemen have created it. They're my favorite guys. I just like big ol' guys. Hey, maybe because I'm a big ol' guy who was once a big ol' offensive tackle, so I know how offensive linemen never get much attention. It's always the guys who ran with the ball or threw the ball. The guys that did the blocking are never mentioned except when the referee throws his flag, stands facing the television camera, and turns on his microphone.

"Holding, number seventy-nine," he'll say.

I always thought that if the referee announced a holding penalty, then when number seventy-nine made a good block, the referee should turn on his microphone and say, "Hey, number seventy-nine pancaked his man. That's why the running back got through there." So ever since I've had a microphone in the television booth, I've tried to tell the viewers about offensive linemen. All the viewers see the guy who runs with the ball or the guy who throws the ball and the guy who catches the ball, but I like to point out the big ol' linemen who let those other guys run, throw, and catch.

Years ago most football people thought that 300 pounds was too big for an offensive lineman. There were some 300-pounders like Roger Brown and Ernie Ladd, but they were defensive linemen. On offense, even if a guy weighed 300, he was listed at 290 in the program. Coaches wanted more height, more speed, but not more weight. Joe Jacoby was one of the first great 300-pounders on the offensive line.

Hey, those 300-pounders do eat a lot. Anyone can get big just by eating a lot. But if you eat a lot, you usually get fat and slow and you don't have any endurance. But these big guys not only can move, they have stamina and endurance. You never see 'em get tired. The most important quarter is the fourth quarter. You have to have stamina and endurance in the fourth quarter, but I've never seen the Cowboys' offensive line get tired.

"We're three hundred pounds," Nate keeps telling me, "but we can dance."

Nate knows football. He taught me to appreciate a little subtle thing Mark Stepnoski did as the Cowboys' center before he joined the Oilers in 1995 as a free agent. Like every left guard, Nate worries about his defensive man getting through between him and the center. If a guard lets his man hit that inside gap, that man is really right in the quarterback's face. Mark Stepnoski would snap the ball with his right hand, then put up his left hand in that gap between Nate and him. Defensive guys are always attacking a center's right shoulder, so Mark had to learn to protect that snap hand too. He was so quick, he could get his left hand up to close that gap next to Nate, then protect that snap hand by stepping to his right.

After Nate told me about it, I watched Mark and I thought, "Holy moly, how does he do that?" But if a center doesn't do that, there's a big gap between him and the left guard.

I thought the Cowboys would really miss Mark Stepnoski, but they signed Ray Donaldson, who soon got tired of hearing and reading that he was taking Mark's place. Ray had been a four-time Pro Bowl center with the Colts before anchoring the Seahawks' offensive line. When he joined the Cowboys he was thirty-seven, but his three hundred pounds impressed Nate Newton right away.

"Ray's got old-man strength," Nate informed me.

"What do you mean, old-man strength?" I asked.

"You know how as a kid," Nate said, "no matter what you lifted or what you did, your old man was always stronger than you. That's old-man strength. That's what Ray Donaldson has. He's just like your old man."

Nate was also the first to tell me that Erik Williams would be an All-Pro tackle.

Not many people had heard of Erik when the Cowboys drafted him in the third round in 1991 out of Central State, a small Ohio college. But as soon as Erik got to training camp, the Cowboys veterans knew he was something special. The first time I saw Nate that year, he pointed across the locker room at this huge rookie.

"See that kid," Nate said. "His name is Erik Williams and he's going to be a great player. You're going to be talking about him."

Nate's like that. He just wanted me to know. I started watching Erik; and by 1993, he was just overpowering, just devastating. When he's healthy, Erik is the NFL's best offensive lineman now.

Every offensive tackle worries about a pass rusher's inside move, but Erik can handle the inside better than anybody else. If a pass rusher tries to go around the outside, the tackle can push him outside. If a pass rusher comes straight at him, the tackle is usually too strong for him. But if a pass rusher tries to come inside, the tackle has to keep his inside foot up. If he opens that inside foot, the pass rusher has a straight lane to the quarterback.

As the right tackle pass blocking against the defensive left end, Erik keeps his outside foot, his right foot, back a little. That lets the pass rusher go outside, but that's what Erik wants him to do.

If the pass rusher tries to go to the inside, Erik keeps his inside foot, his left foot, up a little and the pass rusher can't get inside him. To protect that inside even more, Erik learned to throw his left arm and straighten up the pass rusher. In a 1993 game, Steve Emtman of the Colts tried an inside move, but Erik just drove him into the Hoosier Dome carpet.

In the 1995 NFC championship game, Erik leveled the Packers' nose tackle, John Jurkovic, with what some people mistakenly described as an illegal chop-block. But it was a legal block, what coaches call a sprint-cutoff block, a polite phrase for a legal clip.

On a Cowboy sweep to their left against the Packers, right guard Larry Allen pulled and ran left as Erik Williams sprinted to his left and hit Jurkovic from behind. Jurkovic went down with a torn ligament in his left knee. But there was no penalty. Erik's block had been legal. Offensive linemen can use the sprint-cutoff block in an invisible box that extends 3 yards on each side of the line of scrimmage from tackle to tackle.

What I don't understand, and I began arguing this back when I was the Raiders' coach, is why you're allowed to clip a defensive nose tackle or a defensive tackle inside that invisible box, but you're not allowed to clip anybody else outside it. You can't do it to a defensive end or a linebacker. You can't do it to a defensive back. You can't do it on a punt return. You can't do it on a kickoff return.

To call the sprint-cutoff block a legal clip is an oxymoron. It's either a clip and it's illegal or you ought to be able to clip anywhere on the field. To be able to do something illegal in one area but nowhere else doesn't make sense.

Clipping is not only illegal, it's dangerous. But the NFL has a legal zone, that tackle-to-tackle box, for an illegal play. Why is it legal to clip a nose tackle or a defensive tackle in that box, but you can't clip anybody else anywhere else?

Years ago the chop-block was legal too, but now it's illegal. Here's how to understand the difference between the chop-block and the sprint-cutoff block: If Larry Allen were fighting off John Jurkovic's rush, Larry and John would have been "engaged," to use the game officials' terminology. In that situation, where two linemen are engaged, if Erik Williams had blocked John from behind, it would have been an illegal block. Fifteen yards.

Not many offensive linemen can dominate a game. The good ones pass block well and run block well. But the term *dominate* is usually reserved for a quarterback like Joe

Montana or Dan Marino or John Elway or Steve Young, for a running back like Emmitt Smith, for a linebacker like Lawrence Taylor or Dick Butkus.

You hardly ever use that term for an offensive lineman, but Erik Williams can dominate a game. One time Erik's man hit Troy Aikman late. Erik beat up on the guy so much after that, the other team had to take him out. Erik is listed at 324 pounds, but he's got to be 340, maybe 350; and at six feet six, he's so tall, so massive, he can use it all.

When you think of dominant offensive linemen or dominant offensive lines, they usually have a dominant running back, like the Cowboys have with Emmitt Smith, or the Redskins had with John Riggins when their offensive line was known as "The Hogs."

Joe Gibbs, the coach of those Redskins, is in the Hall of Fame now for winning three Super Bowls with three different quarterbacks (Joe Theismann, Doug Williams, and Mark Rypien). That only goes to prove my theory that three of The Hogs were the common denominator of those three Super Bowl wins—Joe Jacoby at left tackle, Russ Grimm at left guard, and Jeff Bostic at center. To me, Jacoby and Grimm should be in the Hall of Fame someday. But as huge as those Hogs were, they're not as huge as the Cowboys' offensive linemen. Including left tackle Mark Tuinei, listed at 314 pounds, and center Derek Kennard at 333 (he replaced Ray Donaldson, out with a fractured right ankle), the total listed weight of the Cowboys' line in Super Bowl XXX was 1,617 pounds, probably closer to 1,700 pounds in actual weight. That's heavier than a three-quarter-ton pickup truck.

You can be huge as long as you're quick and fast. Maybe the fastest offensive lineman now, at least for his weight, is Larry Allen, the Cowboys' right guard who's listed at 326 pounds. In a game in New Orleans during the 1994 season, Darion Conner, a 245-pound linebacker, intercepted a pass at the Saints' 29-yard line and appeared on his way to a touchdown, until Larry chased him down from across the field and tackled him at the 15. He's so aggressive, he plays as if he were a defensive lineman.

To be a good offensive lineman, you've got to be aggressive. Some people think offensive linemen should be passive, especially when they're blocking pass rushers. Yes, pass blocking is passive in that you have to accept the other guy's charge and keep yourself between him and your quarterback, but that doesn't mean an offensive lineman can't be aggressive. If he's going to get the job done, he's got to be aggressive.

There are more and more 300-pound offensive linemen now, but you don't need to be 300 pounds to be a great one. At least you don't if you're Anthony Munoz, the Bengals' tackle who played in eleven consecutive Pro Bowls, the NFL record. He was listed at 278, but at six feet six, he looked almost lean. The first time I saw him, I was visiting my boyhood pal John Robinson, then the USC coach in his first time around there. John took me down to where some of his players were working out.

"I want to show you this freshman," John said.

The next thing I knew, this huge kid was not only standing in the doorway, he filled the doorway.

"You ought to see the way he moves," John said.

John had never seen Anthony play football in high school, but when he heard that Anthony played basketball, he went to a game.

"Just from the way he moved," John told me, "I offered him a football scholarship."

As a pass protector, Anthony Munoz was one of the best. He had great balance, great feet. He was so good that most people took him for granted. But that shouldn't happen. When an offensive lineman gets the job done, give him as much credit as you'd give him blame if he didn't get the job done. Bubba Paris taught me that.

Before a 49ers game with the Giants several years ago, Bubba walked over to talk to me about his having to block Lawrence Taylor.

"I want you to do me a favor," Bubba said. "If Lawrence Taylor beats me, you go ahead and replay that and chalkboard that all you want and run it back and forth. You do all those things. But when I block him, I hope you show that too."

Bubba was right. Don't just credit the pass rusher when he gets to the quarterback. Be sure to credit the offensive lineman when that pass rusher doesn't get to the quarterback.

As big as offensive linemen are, they wear jerseys three to four sizes too small. They want the jersey to be so tight the pass rusher won't have anything to grab. They started wearing those tight jerseys after the head slap was outlawed. Deacon Jones, a Rams defensive end in their "Fearsome Foursome," popularized the head slap about a quarter of a century ago. In pass blocking, an offensive lineman is always trying to stay square, and the pass rusher is always trying to take him out of square. Pass rushers could do that with the head slap. The pass blocker's head would turn and that would turn his power, then the pass rusher would use a swim move to get by him.

When the pass rushers couldn't use the head slap anymore, they started grabbing the loose jersey around the offensive lineman's shoulders. So the linemen started wearing tighter jerseys.

At first some linemen used tape that was sticky on both sides. They would stick it against the front of their shoulder pads, then they would flatten their jersey against the other sticky side.

The first offensive linemen I ever saw do that were Jackie Slater and his Rams teammates. I never stop by a locker room before a game now, because I talk to the players the day before. But in my early years as a broadcaster, I liked to go to the locker room and just sit around with the "early birds," the players who always got there ahead of most of their teammates. Then as now, I gravitated to the offensive linemen; and if the Rams were playing, that meant Jackie Slater.

"I always worried," Jackie told me years later, "that when we were using that two-sided tape, you were sitting there talking to us and watching us; and if it were illegal, you might mention it on the air."

It wasn't illegal, but I guess Jackie wasn't sure, and he wasn't about to ask if it was. I don't think I ever mentioned it on the air anyway. But offensive linemen soon found a better way to keep pass rushers from grabbing their jerseys. They sprayed silicone on their jerseys and still do. It's illegal but if the officials know it, they never seem to do anything about it.

Jim Burt still laughs about this. When he was the 49ers' nose tackle, he was deactivated for a game for some reason. But when he was on the sideline we had a shot of him spraying silicone on the 49ers' jerseys.

Most offensive linemen were born to play football and to play it as long as they can, like Stan Brock. When he got to Super Bowl XXIX with the Chargers, that was his fifteenth season. His brother, Pete, was the same way. As the Patriots' first-round choice in 1976, he was their center for twelve years. I'm sure they got that from their father up there in the Oregon woods. At a Chargers practice one day, their dad grabbed me and barked, "How you doin'?" like a cowboy would, like he'd known me all his life.

If some NFL team let a player's dad play now, Stan Brock's dad would probably think he could, just like Stan thinks he can play forever. Nothing bothers a good offensive lineman. Once, before a 1993 playoff game in Giants Stadium, I was talking to the Vikings' Tim Irwin about what football players always talk about late in the season there, the wind and the weather. The quarterbacks and the kickers don't want any wind. The smaller, faster guys always want nice weather so they can stay warm, so they won't pull their hamstrings. But the big guys like Tim Irwin don't care.

"As cold as it gets here in Giants Stadium in the play-offs," I asked Tim before that wild-card game, "at what point does it get too cold to play?"

"For a big lineman," Tim said, "the only way it ever gets too cold to play is if you're standing out there and you spit and the spit freezes before it hits the ground. As long as your spit doesn't freeze before it hits the ground, it's not too cold to play."

To test his theory, I spit, but my spit didn't freeze before it hit the ground. It couldn't have been too cold to play.

Tim Irwin and Stan Brock are throwbacks to the offensive linemen I knew when I was coaching the Raiders, to guys I had like Art Shell, Gene Upshaw, Bob Brown, Henry Lawrence, and Jim Otto. Another throwback is Bruce Matthews, whose father, Clay Sr., was a 49ers linebacker when I was going to Kezar Stadium as a teenager. Since joining the Oilers in 1983 as a first-round choice out of Southern Cal, Bruce has been the NFL's most versatile offensive lineman. He's made the Pro Bowl seven times—four as a center, three as a right guard. He also was a right tackle for one full season, a left tackle for another.

When the Oilers used that run-and-shoot offense with Warren Moon at quarterback, Bruce Matthews made it work with his blocking. With the run-and-shoot, you never have a tight end, so you never get any double-teams. If you don't have any double-teams, it's hard to do any pulling. You limit your combination blocks to so few that all you become is a pass protector. Bruce had to be good in different positions in maybe the most difficult situation for an offensive lineman to be good.

Randall McDaniel is another versatile lineman. When the Vikings are in a short-yardage or goal-line situation, he sometimes lines up at fullback as a lead blocker, but he's basically a guard, an annual Pro Bowl guard. It's hard for some guards to be strong in a small area and still be quick out in an open field. Some guards can pull in order to trap an opposing tackler or to lead the interference through a hole or on a sweep outside, but they miss their blocks. Randall is strong in the small area and when he pulls, he can get out into the open field. And he seldom misses his block.

One of the best blockers was Jay Hilgenberg, the Bears' center on their Super Bowl XX team. At six feet three and 256, he wasn't real big, and he wasn't real strong; but he had great leverage from being a wrestler at the University of Iowa. One of the most important things in blocking is to get underneath the other guy, and he used wrestling techniques to do that. The guy that's the lowest or underneath the other guy's shoulder pads usually wins. The guy that's the highest usually loses. But what made him all-time All-Madden was what he told me one day.

"The greatest thing about being a football player," he said, "is you don't have to take a shower to go to work."

For some reason there don't seem to be as many great offensive linemen as there used to be, but there are a few good young ones, like the Saints' tackle Willie Roaf, the only football player I know who walks on his toes. As big as Willie is at six feet five and 300, he has skinny calf muscles in his legs. And that's something you can't make bigger. You can lift weights twenty-four hours a day, but if you have skinny calves in your legs, they'll stay skinny. You can build up your thighs and your hamstrings, your forearms, your biceps, your shoulders, your neck, but not your calves. You can strengthen your calves, but no matter how much you lift, you can't make 'em bigger.

Back when Willie was a teenager, someone told him, "If you walk on your toes, that flexes your calf muscles and makes 'em bigger." He started walking on his toes.

And he still does. But his calves aren't any bigger now than they were then.

Most offensive linemen aren't worriers, but one of the best, Harris Barton, is the NFL's biggest worrier. If you had an All-Worry team, he'd be the first guy on it. Every time I see him before a 49ers game, he's worrying about how he's playing. He'll ask me, "Did you watch me on film yet? How'd I do? What do you think?"

What I think is that he's one of the best offensive tackles I've ever seen. One of the best guys too.

Early in 1994, with the Olympic torch about to be lit at the Winter Games in Lillehammer, Norway, our opening for the *All-Madden* show was having different people, mostly football players, carrying the All-Madden torch. We had all these people carrying the torch all over the country. But how many guys would come out at eight o'clock in the morning to carry the torch across the Golden Gate Bridge?

Harris Barton did. And he not only carried the torch but wound up just about carrying our producer, Mike Frank.

Mike was out there on the Golden Gate setting it up with Harris and the cameraman. Mike yelled, "Go," and Harris started running, but then Mike made the mistake of looking down at San Francisco Bay from way up there on the walkway with its low railing and the cars buzzing by. The height got him. He went to his knees, then facedown. He was sprawled there while Harris ran across the bridge. Harris had to come back and help Mike wobble off the bridge.

On most teams, the left tackle is more important than the right tackle because most quarterbacks are right-handed and the other team's best pass rusher usually lines up against the left tackle. That way he's rushing from the quarterback's blind side.

But when left-handed Steve Young took over as the 49ers' quarterback, Harris Barton, as their right tackle, had the responsibility of protecting his blind side just as their left tackle, Steve Wallace, earlier had the responsibility of protecting Joe Montana's blind side. Back when Bill Walsh wanted to get some toughness on the 49ers, Steve Wallace was one of the guys who provided it. Steve is a battler. He always reminded me of a boxer, the way he did anything to keep a guy from getting to his quarterback. His problem was that anything sometimes resulted in concussions.

After a CAT scan cleared Steve Wallace of any serious damage, he started wearing a special protective semi-helmet on top of his real helmet. It gave him confidence to stick his head in there again. Your head is the middle of your body. Wherever your head goes, your body is going to go. Your head always has to point in the right direction.

Steve Wallace is another one of the good guys, like most offensive linemen are. The good guys on a team are the stand-up guys who talk to the writers after a loss, especially a tough loss. If you don't know who they are on the team you know best, just read the papers the day after that team loses and see who's quoted. Some players will talk to the writers after a win, but they won't talk after a loss. It's not that the guys who don't talk after a loss are necessarily bad guys, but the writers know there are certain guys they can depend on to talk, no matter what.

Around the 49ers, one of those good guys is Jesse Sapolu. When the 49ers lose, Jesse Sapolu always stands up at his locker and talks about it. Another reason big ol' offensive linemen are my favorite guys.

THE MINISTER
AND L.T.

Reggie White was steaming. His Packers were about to be beaten by the Cowboys, 34–24, early in the 1995 season; and on the sideline, he was growling in his hoarse voice at some of his defensive teammates.

"Every time we play these guys," I could hear him saying on my monitor, "they kick our tails."

During a game you're not going to hear many players refer to people's backsides as tails, but Reggie White does. As an ordained minister who's known as the "Minister of Defense," he doesn't curse and he doesn't like to hear anybody else curse.

That's just another dimension to Reggie White, the best defensive lineman I've seen as a broadcaster.

What makes Reggie special is that he's got the combination that every coach is looking for in a defensive lineman, but seldom finds—speed, size, and strength. He's been timed for 40 yards at 4.6 seconds. Hey, that's what some wide receivers are timed at, what some defensive backs are timed at. Until recently, defensive linemen were never timed at 4.6, especially somebody who is as big and thick as Reggie is at six feet five and 300 pounds, if not more.

Over the years, the difference in both defensive and offensive linemen is the number of 300-pounders. At one time 300-pound guys could just waddle. Then some of them could run a little, maybe 5.5 seconds for 40 yards. Now some are running 4.6.

Other guys who were big and strong could never run like Reggie, and the guys who could run a little, like Bubba Smith, weren't as strong as Reggie. Most people think of Reggie as a pass rusher because he holds the NFL career record for sacks, but some of his biggest plays have been against the run. When the Packers held Barry Sanders to minus one yard in thirteen carries for the Lions in a 1994 wild-card playoff, Reggie was the reason. Sometimes he lined up at defensive end, sometimes at defensive tackle; and wherever Barry went, Reggie was there to tackle him or stack up his blockers so another Packer could tackle him.

What makes Reggie the best is that he can play anywhere. He can line up over the tight end, over the offensive tackle, over the offensive guard, over the center.

"I like that," he told me. "Players think that the defensive ends are the athletes and the defensive tackles are the men. I feel honored. I'm an athlete and a man."

He sure is. No matter where Reggie lines up, he's got that move that most people call "the Hump," where he gets underneath a pass blocker, lifts him, and throws him. In a 1994 Thanksgiving Day game in Dallas, he just lifted 325-pound rookie guard Larry Allen off his feet and rushed the passer. Sometime later I mentioned to Reggie that Howie Long had talked about that move on Fox's pregame show and showed how Reggie did it.

"Howie called it 'the Hump,'" I said.

"That's strange, because I call it 'the Howie,'" Reggie said. "The first time I ever saw that move Howie Long did it when he was with the Raiders. I tried it, and it worked, so I called it 'the Howie.'"

Whatever you call it, Reggie does it all. Line up outside or inside. Rush the passer. Play the run. Take on a double-team.

People tell me the Bills' Bruce Smith does it all too. And even with the little I see of him, I know he's a great defensive end. But as good a pass rusher as he is, he doesn't line up in as many different places as Reggie does and I don't think he has Reggie's strength.

Strictly as a pass rusher, Charles Haley is the best around now. He's a disruptive force that can take over a game.

As the first player to earn five Super Bowl rings (three with the Cowboys after two with the 49ers), Charles makes everyone around him better. He runs in there like a bowling ball hitting the pins. Bodies start flying. Even if they put two blockers on him, that means somebody else is free to go after the passer. He's agile. He's tough. He's quick. He's got strong hands. And the minute the other team thinks he's just a pass rusher, he'll stack up the run.

Charles is also a thinker. When he was recuperating from spinal disk surgery late in the 1995 season, the Cowboys moved Leon Lett from tackle to end.

"They're different positions," Charles told him. "Don't play end like you play tackle. Don't just bull rush. Use your quickness. Use your moves."

In the continuing changes of defensive football, Charles Haley and Bruce Smith are each now the primary pass rusher in a four-man line, just as Lawrence Taylor was the primary pass rusher as an outside linebacker behind a three-man line.

Not that Haley or Smith are what L.T. was. Maybe nobody ever will be. Just as Joe Montana is the most dominant offensive player I've seen in my years in the television booth, L.T. is the most dominant defensive player. He

didn't have to lead the Giants to two Super Bowl championships for me to know that. All the quarterbacks who
had to play against him let me know that, not in so many
words as in so many glances. Whenever those quarterbacks were playing the Giants, the first thing they did as
the huddle broke was glance to see where L.T. was lined
up. He was usually to their left, but sometimes he was to
their right. Wherever he was, the quarterback had to know
where he was because if he wasn't where they expected
him to be, it meant the quarterback would need to audible
to a different play or a different pass protection. All the
quarterbacks began glancing to see where he was as soon
as he arrived in 1981 out of North Carolina as the second
player taken in that year's college draft.

"When I first came into the league," he once told me, "I
felt no one could play with me. I felt I was in control of
every ball game, every situation. I knew what I was doing
in my mind. I knew my body was superior to a lot of different people, a lot of people in general."

He wasn't bragging. He wasn't trying to con me or anybody else. He didn't have to. He just knew that he knew
how to play football better than anybody else on defense.
He quickly proved it. His second year, the Giants were in the
Thanksgiving Day game in the Silverdome as the Lions took
a 6–0 lead. But in the second half, he blitzed Gary Danielson
into hurrying a pass that Harry Carson intercepted, setting
up a Giants field goal. On the Lions' next series, he forced
Billy Sims's fumble that the Giants recovered, setting up
another field goal. On the Lions' next series, he sacked
Danielson with one hand, forcing a punt. When the Lions
threatened to break the 6–6 tie by driving to the 4-yard line,
he picked off Danielson's pass into the flat and ran 97 yards
for a touchdown and a 13–6 win.

"There's only one defensive player that can win a football game and that was you," I once told him. "I thought
you won that game."

And tough, I don't know of anybody any tougher than L.T. was. Not wild tough like Dick Butkus was, but a quieter tough when he had to be.

Before the Giants went to Philadelphia in 1987, the Eagles' coach, Buddy Ryan, told the New York writers, "The only player that can catch Randall Cunningham is number fifty-six"—meaning L.T.—"and I'm not sure he can do it this year." When the writers asked number fifty-six about Buddy's comment, he shrugged it off, but he remembered. In the final seconds of that game, with the Giants protecting a 20–17 lead, Cunningham took off for the right sideline on third down and appeared on his way to a first down. From across the field, L.T. was chasing him when he suddenly appeared to take what racehorse people call a bad step.

L.T. had pulled the hamstring muscle in his right leg. Almost any other player would have fallen or at least limped. He not only kept running, he caught Cunningham and tackled him a yard short of the first down.

When the Eagles missed a long field goal, L.T.'s tackle had preserved the Giants' win. He hobbled off the field to the locker room, then hobbled into the trainer's room and stretched out on a rubbing table. When Bill Parcells came over to see how he was, he looked up at the Giants' coach.

"I guess I can still catch him," he said.

The next year in New Orleans he won another game almost all by himself despite a torn shoulder muscle. Wearing a brace that he adjusted whenever he came to the sideline, he had three sacks, two forced fumbles, and ten tackles in a 13–12 win. Late in the 1989 season the Giants were in San Francisco on a Monday night, when he suddenly screamed in pain and toppled to the grass. He had to be taken off the field on a cart. His injury appeared to be a severely sprained right ankle, then X rays showed a hairline fracture of the tibia in his right leg near the ankle. When he was asked, "Are you out for the season?" he just glared.

"Are you kiddin'?" he said.

He played the first half of the following Sunday's game before his painkillers wore off, sat out the next game, then played the last two games of the season and a wild-card playoff game.

All on a broken right leg.

When the Giants won the 1990 NFC championship in San Francisco on their way to winning Super Bowl XXV, he was involved in a play you hardly ever see. If the 49ers could run out the clock, they would win, 13–12, and have a chance to be the first team to win three Super Bowls in a row, but the Giants' Erik Howard made the best play I've ever seen a nose tackle make. In stopping a run up the middle, he somehow forced Roger Craig to fumble. The ball popped up and L.T. snatched it out of the air at the Giants' 42-yard line with three minutes and forty-three seconds left. The Giants won, 15–13, on Matt Bahr's 42-yard field goal as time expired.

With so many teams now using a four-man front and three linebackers, the L.T. type of linebacker, the pass-rushing outside linebacker behind a three-man line, is an endangered species.

When the Steelers got to Super Bowl XXX as the 1995 AFC champions, they were one of the few teams still using four linebackers. The Steelers' outside linebackers, Greg Lloyd and Kevin Greene, were basically pass rushers like L.T. was. With both Lloyd and Greene coming at the quarterback nearly all the time, the Steelers were a tough team, not a finesse team. But when a linebacker, like any other player, moves to another team as a free agent, as Ken Norton Jr. did from the Cowboys to the 49ers in 1994, sometimes he needs time to adjust to new teammates and a new system.

When the 49ers won Super Bowl XXIX in Ken's first season there, he wasn't as effective as he had been with the Cowboys in winning the two previous Super Bowls.

Even though the 49ers got knocked out of the playoffs in 1995, he was a better linebacker because he had adjusted to the people around him and the system.

Junior Seau is another strong linebacker. When I watched the Chargers practice against the 49ers during training camp in 1994, he and Jerry Rice were playing up there on another level. They were doing things other players couldn't do. If you go to a Chargers game, you don't need a program to know which one Junior Seau is. But with the rules now favoring the passing game, the four-man line is there to get after the quarterback quickly. You're not going to get as many sacks because the quarterback doesn't hold the ball long enough. With that quick three-step, five-step rhythm passing, a pass rusher doesn't have much time to get to the quarterback.

The coaches' word is no longer *rush*. It's *push*. They want their four defensive linemen to push the pocket, to get their hands in the quarterback's face.

With that rhythm passing, your pass rushers don't have time to get to the quarterback, so they have to be able to take away the passing lanes. If the quarterback goes one-two-three throw, those big pass rushers have to get their hands up. Make the quarterback throw over trees. That's where the Cowboys' Leon Lett is so good. He's six six, and when he gets his long arms up, he looks like he's nine nine.

Most of the best defensive linemen now are inside guys, like Leon Lett, the 49ers' Dana Stubblefield and Bryant Young, the Raiders' Chester McGlockton, the Chiefs' Dan Saleaumua, the Seahawks' Cortez Kennedy, and Arizona's Eric Swann.

With the switch to the four-man line, every team is trying to find the big defensive end, the big outside pass rushers like Deacon Jones and Gino Marchetti, who played when the four-man line was popular years ago. In that era, the dominant player against the run was the middle linebacker, especially Dick Butkus, Ray Nitschke, and Sam Huff.

Mike Singletary, the Bears' middle linebacker on their Super Bowl XX team, might have been the last of those middle linebackers. He called the defenses. He made all the adjustments. He was smart, emotional, and tough. That's a combination you don't see very often. Matt Millen was that type too—wild, fiery, smart, tough, loved to play, loved to tackle. Wherever he went, to Penn State, to the Raiders, to the 49ers, to the Redskins, they won. What I always liked about Matt was that when someone really hit him or he really hit someone, he'd laugh. When he played behind a three-man line he was an inside linebacker. And when he played behind a four-man line he was a middle linebacker. If he had played in that Butkus–Nitschke–Huff era, he would've been a dominant middle linebacker.

But with so much passing now, you don't need that dominant middle linebacker against the run, and when a team goes to its nickel defense against the pass, the middle linebacker usually comes out for a defensive back. Reggie White, Charles Haley, Bruce Smith, and the Chiefs' Neil Smith can rush the passer, but there aren't a lot of great pass-rushing defensive ends. The young defensive end now is better playing inside at defensive tackle.

When you talk about defensive ends as pure pass rushers, I think Richard Dent was the best, whenever he wanted to be the best. When he was with the Bears team that swept through Super Bowl XX with an 18–1 record, he played at three levels as a pass rusher. One was just okay, two was good, and three was unblockable. When he played at that unblockable level, Richard was the best pass rusher as a defensive end that I've seen in my years as a broadcaster.

But after the coaches started using a three-man line, the real defensive ends got lost. They called them defensive ends; but in a three-man line, you're really playing with three tackles, and one of your outside linebackers is your pass rusher, like L.T. was. But even with some good linebackers, there's nobody around now who's even close to dominating defense like L.T. did. I realized that when Deion Sanders was named the NFL's Defensive Player of the Year in 1994. Until then the defensive player of the year was always a lineman or a linebacker, but suddenly it was a cornerback. Not that Deion didn't deserve the award. He did. That season there was no linebacker or lineman that was a dominating player.

Then in 1995 things got back to normal. Bryce Paup, the Bills' linebacker, got the award. I liked that. As much as I admire Deion Sanders as a cornerback, linebackers and linemen are the heart of every team's defense.

I wish defense was recognized more. If there's a low-scoring game in football or basketball or a 0–0 game in baseball, too many people think it's boring, when they should be appreciating good defense or good pitching. It's like defense isn't even there. Look at Hakeem Olajuwon, the Houston Rockets' great center. He plays just as hard at the defensive end of the court as he does at the offensive end. Look at Greg Maddux, the Atlanta Braves' right-hander, or Randy Johnson, the Seattle Mariners' left-hander. They may not sell as many sneakers and hamburgers as the quarterbacks or basketball's top scorers or baseball's home-run hitters, but they deserve to be recognized for playing defense the way it's supposed to be played.

Next to offensive linemen, defensive linemen and linebackers are my favorite guys. Some are even throwbacks.

One of those throwbacks is Chris Spielman, who's with the Bills now and who once scored an unusual touchdown for the Lions. He yanked the ball out of the hands of Bears tight end Chris Gedney, ran 25 yards into the end zone, dropped to his knees, and touched the ball to the ground with both hands. Sort of a throwback spike.

"That's the way you had to do it in the early days of pro football," he later explained. "I did it as a tribute to all the men who played in those years."

He also helped the Lions score touchdowns. When their offense was in a goal-line or short-yardage situation, he sometimes lined up as a blocking back. Whenever I did a Lions game, I always enjoyed talking to him after practice because he really knows football. He wants to be a coach someday, and he'll be a good one. But he's fidgety. One time I was talking to him after practice, when he started pulling at one of his sneakers where the rubber strip meets the sole. When he couldn't get it off with his hands, he bit it off. Then he started chewing it like a piece of gum.

That's my kind of guy. My kind of linebacker. My kind of throwback.

DOUBLE-DUTY DEION

No matter what he's doing, Deion Sanders is always different. One day when he was with the 49ers, I noticed he was covering Jerry Rice in practice with his hands behind his back.

"It makes me concentrate on my footwork," he told me.

Deion has never done that in a game, but someday he might, if only because you never know what he might do. Or what he can do, like be a wide receiver too. Some people just think he's Neon Deion, Prime Time, with a seven-year $35 million contract. They might think he's all talk, but he can play. He deserves that big contract because he's the NFL's best cornerback. And maybe one of its best wide receivers.

Some people in the Cowboys organization think that, instead of Deion playing cornerback and spotting as a wide receiver, he should be a wide receiver and spot as a cornerback.

The Cowboys learned in 1995 that even as a spot player on offense, Deion made a difference. When the Cowboys' coaches analyzed their 20–17 loss in Philadelphia that is remembered mostly for Dallas not getting a first down on fourth and one at the Eagles' 29-yard line, they realized that when Deion lined up as a wide receiver, it opened up their running game.

When the Eagles were double-covering both Michael Irvin and Deion during the first half, Emmitt Smith ran for 98 yards as the Cowboys took a 17–6 lead. When Deion wasn't used much on offense in the second half, the Eagles kept that linebacker in there, shut Emmitt down, and the Cowboys didn't score again.

During his nine regular-season games, Deion lined up for an offensive snap a total of only twenty-three times, including eight in that Eagles game. At first the Cowboys' coaches believed they had to have a play for him if he was in there as a wide receiver. But in that Eagles game, they realized they could still run their other plays. In their three postseason games, Deion lined up nearly twice as often, a total of forty-two snaps: thirteen against the Eagles, seventeen against the Packers, twelve against the Steelers.

In the Cowboys offense, lining up is only the beginning. Troy Aikman is a perfectionist, and their passing game is all timing. Troy has to know not just that Deion is going to run a certain pattern, but he's got to know precisely where Deion will be on that certain pattern when Troy's back foot hits the turf in his five-step drop.

Now that Deion won't be playing baseball, he'll be able to get a foundation of both the offense and the defense in training camp. He'll develop the timing he'll need as a wide receiver. Since he's a man-to-man cornerback, he'll be able to spend more time with the offense.

If anybody can play both ways in the NFL now, Deion can. All those people who are quick to knock him, they don't want to know that he's a hard worker, that he's a good guy, that he goes home to his wife and kids like most pro football players do. They think he's just gifted and flashy. And he is, but he works hard. Like he will in wanting to be a wide receiver. Like he does in covering pass receivers in practice with his hands behind his back.

"Sometimes I have to stick my hands out for balance," he told me, "but I don't put my hands on the receiver at all."

When an athlete gets tired, the first thing that goes is his legs. If his legs are tired, his feet won't move as quickly. You can always tell if a boxer is tired by looking at his legs. It's the same thing with a football player. He needs that quickness in his legs, especially a defensive back.

His legs are why Deion was able to play two major-league sports like Bo Jackson did. In the years when Deion joined the Falcons after his baseball season, their player personnel director, Ken Herock, who was once one of my Raiders' tight ends, couldn't get over how quickly Deion adjusted.

"Deion," Ken told me, "is the only football player I've ever seen who doesn't need time to get ready. He can walk in off the street and play right away. No training camp. No practice. Just put on his uniform and play."

Not just play, but play cornerback better than anybody else. When he joined the Cowboys about a third of the way through the 1995 season, he wasn't quite ready to do that because he had needed arthroscopic surgery on his left ankle to fix a baseball injury. While recuperating, he hadn't been able to do his running. Then he pulled a hamstring in his first game, then he aggravated it in the Thanksgiving Day game.

But by the playoffs, he was almost as fast as ever. And he helped the Cowboys win what Jerry Jones got him to win, Super Bowl XXX.

To me, Deion just might be the fastest defensive player ever. He's not just fast, he's football fast. When some fast guys put on a football uniform, with all the pads and tape, they slow down. But when Deion puts on his football uniform, he doesn't slow down. If anything, he seems to get faster. No matter how fast you think you're going in trying to catch him, he'll go faster. No matter how fast you're going in trying to run away from him, he'll catch you. No matter how far the ball is thrown, he's going to catch up to it. Put all the fast NFL players in a race in their football uniforms, he would be the fastest guy.

I've been around some great cornerbacks. I coached Willie Brown and coached against Mel Blount. I coached Lester Hayes and I've seen Mike Haynes, who together had the best Super Bowl any pair of cornerbacks ever had. When the Raiders beat the Redskins, 38–9, in Super Bowl XVIII, I've never seen two cornerbacks play better than those two did. To me, that's the criterion. Not only being able to play and to play well, but to excel in big games.

But none of those great cornerbacks had Deion's speed. He's just a special athlete. He's so quick, he's probably the best cover cornerback that's ever played. Not many people know that at Florida State, he was not only an All-America cornerback and the centerfielder on the baseball team, he also qualified as a 100-meter sprinter for the 1988 Olympic Trials. He's so fast, he baits you to throw deep because he wants to intercept. He thinks like an offensive player.

Deion is trying to put a reverse spin on being a cornerback. He doesn't want to be thought of as just another cornerback who has to "watch out, you're covering . . ." Jerry Rice or Herman Moore or Robert Brooks or Isaac Bruce. He wants those wide receivers to be thinking, *Watch out, Deion Sanders is covering you.*

I hear people say, "Deion's not physical," but he's a very physical cornerback when he's covering a receiver. I hear people say, "He doesn't tackle," but if there's a tackle that has to be made, he'll make it. He prides himself on a game when he doesn't have to make a tackle. If you're a corner and you shut out your man without him catching a pass, you might not make a tackle because the other team probably hasn't thrown much in your area. The way the Cowboys play, and the way the 49ers played when Deion was there, the safety is the force tackler: Darren Woodson with the Cowboys, Tim McDonald with the 49ers.

I hear people say, "I'd make Deion tackle, I'd run at him." But you can't run at him. Their defense doesn't let you. That's not what he's called on to do. With a piece of chalk and a chalkboard, some people might think they can exploit Deion's tackling, but on the field they can't.

I hear people say, "If Deion is so fast, why don't the Cowboys use him in a cornerback blitz once in a while?" But he's the cornerback that allows the Cowboys to blitz a safety or another cornerback because he can cover the other team's best wide receiver man to man all over the field.

With his blue do-rag under his helmet, with his music albums and videos, with his fast talk, Deion is easy for some people to dislike; but whenever I've been around him with the Cowboys, the 49ers, and the Falcons, he has always seemed like a guy who is really respected by his teammates. At practice or in the locker room he's always talking to other players, always having fun with them. And they're always talking to him, always having fun with him.

I know about Jerry Rice's problems with Deion, but I never felt any of that was personal.

When the Cowboys signed Deion in 1995 and the 49ers didn't, Jerry blasted the writers who were saying that the 49ers wouldn't win the Super Bowl now that the Cowboys had Deion, but Jerry wasn't criticizing Deion so much as defending the 49ers' chances, especially their defensive backs like Tim McDonald, Merton Hanks, and Eric Davis. And when Deion missed the 49ers' Wednesday-night curfew in Miami before Super Bowl XXIX, Jerry and Coach George Seifert got on Deion and several other 49ers who had missed that curfew, but Deion kept his cool.

"This was only Wednesday night, not Saturday night," he said. "And we're still playing the Chargers."

Six weeks earlier the 49ers had routed the Chargers,

38–15, in San Diego; and they would rout the Chargers again, 49–26, in that Super Bowl. But when the 49ers stunned the Cowboys, 38–20, during the 1995 season, Jerry Rice had a right to say that the 49ers were still the champions until the Cowboys with Deion beat them (or, as it turned out, until the Packers beat the 49ers in the playoffs). But with Deion at cornerback, the Cowboys' other defensive backs had to adjust to doing different things on defense, just as the 49ers' defensive backs had to adjust to doing different things after he joined them in 1994.

Deion is such a great man-to-man cover guy, it's a waste to use him in a zone defense. That's like making a racehorse a plow horse. So when the 49ers put Jerry Rice in the slot, the Cowboys couldn't put Deion on him because they needed Deion and their other cornerback, Larry Brown, out there on the two outside receivers.

If the 49ers had lined up in a regular formation with two outside receivers, a tight end, and two running backs, Deion would've taken one wide receiver, and the Cowboys would've zoned the other side. But with Jerry Rice in the slot with two outside receivers, the Cowboys had to play man-to-man or had to adjust their zones to the different formations. That's how you get mismatches. That's how the 49ers took advantage of Jerry coming out of the slot against a linebacker; but I was surprised the Cowboys were surprised when Jerry was in the slot.

During Jerry Rice's early years, the word was that the bump-and-run was a problem for him, that he had trouble getting away from the bump by the cornerback at the line of scrimmage. So the 49ers started moving him around. By putting him in the slot, he was back off the line of scrimmage, so he couldn't be bumped at the line. They also put him in motion, which meant the guy that was supposed to bump him had to come across the field with him and usually was just enough behind him so that he couldn't be bumped. The 49ers had done that for five years.

Some people wondered how the 49ers had used Deion when the other team put its best wide receiver in the slot. The 49ers put a linebacker on him just like the Cowboys did, but because the 49ers have Jerry Rice, they didn't have to worry about the other team's best wide receiver being Jerry Rice.

Hey, Deion's not infallible. In Super Bowl XXX, the Steelers scored on a 6-yard pass to Yancey Thigpen across the middle. Deion started to go in there, then stopped. It wasn't the first time. Deion had been burned late in the season by the Eagles' Fred Barnett on that crossing pattern on a two-point conversion. Every coach saw that tape. So until Deion takes away that crossing pattern near the goal line, other teams are going to do that to him.

Coaches know you can't throw an out or an in or an up on Deion, so they don't try that much. Conversely, you can do some things on Deion. It's going to be a short list, but that crossing pattern near the goal line is on top of that list.

So the good news with Deion Sanders is that he's the best cover corner; the bad news is that your whole defense has to adjust to him. You hire him to play man-to-man: to take a receiver and to cover that receiver. Now all your linebackers and other defensive backs must be able to play man-to-man too. If the others play zone while Deion plays man, you're going to have at least one hole in that zone. You can't put a guy in the zone where Deion's playing man, because in essence that would be a double-coverage. So if you run a receiver into the zone where Deion is playing man-to-man, you can run Deion off, run another receiver into that zone, and there won't be another defensive back in that zone.

For all of Deion's skills, Rod Woodson is probably the most complete cornerback now. If you need a cover guy on the corner or in the slot, he'll cover. If you need somebody who's a hard tackler, he'll tackle. If you need one of your defensive backs to blitz, he'll blitz. When you plan your pass protection, you count the defensive linemen and the linebackers, but you never count the defensive backs. So when Woodson lines up in the slot as if he's going to cover the receiver in the slot, then *boom,* when the ball is snapped, he blitzes the quarterback, it usually works. He does it all, including coming back to play for the Steelers in Super Bowl XXX only four months after serious knee surgery.

But as a group, defensive backs don't tackle well anymore. For that matter, neither do linebackers or linemen.

I first noticed sloppy tackling in 1987 after the real players came back from that three-game strike when the clubs used replacement players. At the time I thought that the real players had just missed working on the fundamentals of tackling, but it was atrocious the rest of that season. It hasn't gotten any better.

My theory is that practicing offensive plays and defensive coverages has become so time-consuming not only during the season but also in training camp, that there's no time for fundamentals. Not just tackling, but also things like the stance, the start, the pass-blocking footwork for the offensive linemen, the ball handling for the quarterbacks.

If you don't have time to practice tackling, then go find good natural tacklers. As the Raiders' coach I hated missed tackles. After one season of poor tackling, we went into the draft with the idea of taking defensive players who were good tacklers. We took Jack Tatum, a safety from Ohio State, in the first round and Phil Villapiano, a linebacker from Bowling Green, in the second round.

To be a good natural tackler, you need good technique and good instincts. You have to know how to wrap the ball carrier, but you have to be able to put yourself in position to wrap him. Some guys know how to tackle, but they can't always get themselves into position to do it. Other guys can get there, but can't tackle. You need the combination of guys who can get there and then tackle.

The ability to cover a pass receiver is how a defensive back coming out of college is evaluated now. His tackling is sometimes ignored. But if a running back breaks through the linebackers or if a pass receiver gets loose, the cornerbacks and safeties are the last line of defense. They need to be good open-field tacklers because there's nothing behind them except the end zone.

You don't necessarily have to hit the ball carrier hard, but you do have to hit him square. It's a matter of staying with his moves. Those running backs and wide receivers don't come at you in a straight line. They're dancing and dipping. Years ago you were taught to watch the ball carrier's belly button. For all his fakes and feints, his belly button won't move that much.

When a defensive back is a good tackler, like Ronnie Lott was, it just adds to his value. It's like having another linebacker.

"Growing up," Ronnie once told me, "I tried to copy my tackling after Jack Tatum. He was the best I've ever seen."

Of all the defensive players I've been around as a broadcaster, Ronnie Lott is the most knowledgeable. He never says, "I've got to see the films." Like any of the really knowledgeable players at any position, he knows the game, and he knows how to play the game. If you have to see the films, if you don't know what happened in a game, you probably didn't know what was happening when it was happening. Ronnie knows the whole picture and he sees the whole picture. He not only knows how to play the game, he knows what it takes to win. What it takes from himself. What it takes from other players. What it takes from coaches.

One day I was talking to Ronnie about assistant coaches who might develop into head coaches.

"I'll tell you who's going to be a good head coach," Ronnie said. "Ray Rhodes."

At the time Ray coached the 49ers' defensive backs, then in 1991 he went to the Packers as Mike Holmgren's defensive coordinator. He returned to the 49ers in 1994 as their defensive coordinator before being named the Eagles' head coach. Now, just as Ronnie Lott predicted, Ray Rhodes is one of the NFL's best young coaches.

Another smart defensive player is Darrell Green, one of the best cover guys even though he's only five feet nine. Not that his height should make any difference. Long before he was the Redskins' first-round choice in 1984 out of Texas A&I, he was a little guy.

I hear people say, "How can Darrell who's five nine cover Michael Irvin who's six three?" But all his life Darrell has been covering guys that are bigger than him, even some who were bigger than Michael. No matter how big they were, Darrell has covered them so well that his size shouldn't even be mentioned anymore.

No matter how good a cornerback is, no matter how quick or how fast, he's going to get beaten every so often. And beaten where everybody can see it. For a big gain. For a touchdown. But he's got to forget it. It's like what I told the Giants' Phillippi Sparks, who is one of the NFL's best young cornerbacks:

"To be a good corner," I said, "you need a bad memory."

But not such a bad memory that you forget that advice.

BILL BATES
IS SPECIAL

Whenever I start talking about special teams, Pat Summerall reminds me of the time that the Cowboys kicked off, the other team's returner fumbled, four or five players jumped on the ball, then Bill Bates leaped on top of the pile.

"When the officials finally dug down through the pile," Pat will say, "Bill Bates had the ball."

That's Bill Bates, my favorite special-teams guy. And when I asked him about how he came up with that fumble, he laughed.

"True story," he said. "You just scratch and claw for that ball with laser-beam determination."

Going into the 1996 season, Bill had been with the Cowboys for thirteen seasons and the captain of their special teams since 1990. But for some reason he's still thought of as an overachiever.

"He's overachieved," says Joe Avezzano, the Cowboys' special-teams coach, "for thirteen seasons."

Bill Bates is an elder statesman now. He's usually at least ten years older, sometimes more, than most of the players on opposing special teams. He discovered that on the Cowboys' kickoff against the Giants in the 1995 season opener. As the players unpiled after the tackle, one of the Giants looked over at him.

"Mr. Bates," he said, "it's really nice to meet you. I've been watching you since the fifth grade."

Mr. Bates didn't appreciate the compliment. When he told Joe Avezzano about it on the sideline, he said, "I told that kid, 'Don't you ever say that to me on the field again.'"

"But it's true," Joe told him.

It's also true that Bill Bates, who is now virtually a player-coach for the Cowboys, has been digging out fumbles and tackling people with that laser-beam determination since he first started playing football for Mullen Methodist Church in Germantown, Tennessee, near Memphis.

"When I was twelve," he told me, "my coach dared me to tackle him. So I did. I hit him so hard, he swallowed his chewing tobacco. Later I saw him puking in the parking lot."

At the University of Tennessee, Bill was a four-year starting safety who was second-team All-Southeastern Conference his junior and senior years, but no NFL team drafted him. Not long after he joined the Cowboys in their 1983 training camp as a free agent, he impressed Coach Tom Landry.

"I hit Tony Dorsett at full speed during a half-speed drill," he remembered. "It knocked poor Tony out."

It also put Bill Bates on the Cowboys, and he's been there ever since. In his second year, he was the first player ever selected for the Pro Bowl as a special-teams player. On kickoffs, he lines up just to the right of the kicker. On punts, he's the punter's personal protector. On kickoff returns, he's near the right sideline in the front five. On punt returns, he's on the far right at the line of scrimmage. But all you really need to know about Bill is that when he and his wife, Denise, had children, they had three. All at once. Triplets. But that didn't stop them. Now they have two more.

I don't see as much of Steve Tasker as I'd like to, but the little I've seen, he's spectacular.

He's only five feet nine and a chunky 181, but he can dunk a basketball two-handed. Now that's an athlete. He's been All-Pro five times. He's been to the Pro Bowl seven times, and in 1993 he was voted its most valuable player, the only special-teams guy ever to get it. On a kickoff, he once tackled Deion Sanders on the 8-yard line. On a kickoff return, he once ran down Rod Woodson from behind. And when the Bills needed a wide receiver late in the 1995 season, he caught fifteen passes for 211 yards and three touchdowns plus another seven for 146 yards in the playoffs.

"If Steve had been a wide receiver his whole career," Jim Kelly said, "he'd be another Steve Largent."

But when Steve was told that his quarterback had compared him to a Hall of Fame wide receiver who caught 819 passes for the Seattle Seahawks, he laughed.

"That's why they drug-test us," he said. "For saying things like that."

As a group, I think the players on special teams are better than ever. Back when I was coaching the Raiders, at the end of the first couple of preseason games, we would put in the guys known as the "others." You had your players and you had the others, who looked like they were the others. They wore number ninety-three or ninety-seven when the numbers only went up to eighty-nine. The others never looked like players. Their shoulders were smaller. Their hips were wider. They just didn't look like pro football players. In recent years I haven't seen many guys on special teams that look like others.

But the special teams are still made up mostly of what I called "fanatics." It used to be that the guys running down under a kickoff or a punt were wilder and more determined than the guys blocking. But the coaches finally figured out, hey, we've got to get guys blocking who are just as wild and determined as the guys running down on coverage.

One reason was that the size of the squad got bigger. The last time I looked, each of the thirty teams had an active list of forty-five players and an inactive list of eight, including a third quarterback who could enter the game if the starter and the backup were injured. With situation substitution, especially with their nickel-and-dime packages, teams started carrying eight defensive backs. Suddenly there were more fast, tough players to fill out the special teams. Another reason was the salary cap. With so many high-priced guys, you need, say, ten minimum-salary guys to make your team as backups at various positions who can also be special-team guys.

If you're a good special-teams player, you can stay in the NFL a long time, like Bill Bates and Steve Tasker.

Each was so good running down to cover kickoffs and punts that the other team used two or sometimes three men to block him at the line of scrimmage. But except for the best cover guys, some blockers on the return team are now usually tougher than the cover guys. Some teams took the tough guys on their coverage teams and put them on the return teams.

Once upon a time, offensive players returned kickoffs and punts, defensive players covered kickoffs and punts. It was always the finesse of the return against the toughness of the coverage. But when the finesse of the return started to get the hell beat out of it, they started putting the toughness of the coverage on the return. Now they're mostly the same guys.

Bill Bates covers the kickoff or a punt, then when the Cowboys are returning a kickoff or a punt, he blocks the other team's toughest guy. That's the difference now. That toughest guy is usually a defensive player. He's good, and he's durable.

As a rule, the good kickoff returner and the good punt returner don't last as long. If you use a rookie running back to return kickoffs and punts and then he develops into a starter, he's become too valuable to risk as a returner. If he's not good enough to be a starter, he's usually not that good of a returner, so you get somebody else to do it. There are exceptions, like Mel Gray, who was with the Lions before going to the Oilers, and David Meggett, who was with the Giants before going to the Patriots.

Other players are too valuable to be used all the time as a return guy, like Darrell Green and Deion Sanders.

Back when Joe Gibbs was the Redskins' coach, I could always tell if, in his mind, it was a really big game. I'd ask him, "Is Darrell Green going to return punts?" If he said yes, I knew it was a really big game. If he said no, I knew he didn't want to risk getting Darrell hurt in what was not a really big game.

The Cowboys used Deion the same way. During the 1995 regular season, he returned only an occasional punt. But in the playoffs and Super Bowl XXX, he was back there waiting for every punt.

Special teams are always important, but in a big game they're even more important, because they can be the difference between two good teams. And more than ever, special-team coaches are more important. Back when I joined the Raiders in 1967 as their linebacker coach, we didn't even have a special-teams coach. I don't think any team did then. The four other assistant coaches (Tom Dahms, Charlie Sumner, Ollie Spencer, and John Polonchek) and I split up the special teams. I was in charge of making sure the right guys went out there on the right special team. After I became the Raiders' head coach in 1969, we still didn't have a special-teams coach until I hired Joe Scanella in 1973. But whenever I spoke at a coaching clinic, I always had a suggestion for the young guys there.

"If you want to get into the NFL," I told them, "start majoring in special teams, because there'll be a time when every team has a special-teams coach. Not only for the kickers and the punters, but for the coverage teams and the return teams."

Years later, Joe Avezzano told me he heard me say that at a clinic. Some teams even have a kicking coach. But except for George Blanda, who was really a quarterback, I don't think I've ever understood kickers or punters unless they played other positions, like Pat Summerall and Lou Groza and other old-timers did.

That's why Pat is usually my All-Madden kicker, although the 1995 team had a ringer—the Clydesdale that kicked an extra point on a Budweiser commercial.

I don't know if Clydesdales get in a rhythm as they prance along, but kickers do. If they lose that rhythm, they're like golfers. They don't know why. Kickers are closer to golfers than they are to football players.

Some kickers are so good now, especially kickers on teams that play their home games in domes, rules are always being proposed to devalue the field goal. One proposal would be to award fewer points the farther the team goes down the field, say, one point from inside the 20-yard line, two points from the 20 to the 29, and three points from the 30 and beyond. I wouldn't like that at all. The farther your offense drives the ball, the easier the field goal should be. The other way, you could just drive the ball for a first down or two, then go for three points. That would be too big an advantage for the dome teams where there's no wind. It would make for a different game.

But there's one proposal I do like—once you're inside the 20, you can't kick a field goal. That would not only make teams go for it on fourth down, it would make teams more aggressive inside the 20 because they would know they can't kick a field goal. Some people wonder if a coach would order his team to take a loss on purpose to get back outside the 20 in order to kick a field goal, but I don't think any coach would have the nerve to do that.

As for punters, with most coaches now, their punter's average yardage, even if it's 42 or 44 yards from the line of scrimmage, isn't as important as his net yardage, meaning the length of his punt minus the yardage gained by the punt returner.

Punting is more of a directional thing now. To compare it to golf, it's more like hitting an iron to a green instead of just hitting your driver as far as you can. More and more coaches want the ball punted to the right or to the left so it lands between the sideline and the numbers, so you can pin the returner to the sideline. Coaches also want the ball to land inside the 20-yard line, so you have a chance of it going out of bounds around the 10 or, even better, inside the 5. But if the ball bounces into the end zone, then it comes out to the 20.

On a punt, the most important thing is hang time. How long it stays in the air. If it stays up there long enough, the returner is either going to fair catch it or let it go. After that, the most important thing is how many punts go out of bounds inside the 20 or can be downed inside the 20.

On kickoffs, every team wants a guy who can boom it through the end zone. That way there's no return and the other team has to start at the 20-yard line. That's really frustrating for the kickoff returner. But even the boomers can't do that every time. So on a kickoff (and a punt), there are three types of returns: to the right, up the middle, and to the left. And they usually depend on where the ball is caught in relation to the yardage numbers near the hash marks on the field.

If you catch the ball on the numbers or between the numbers, you can go where the return was called—left, right, or middle. But if you catch the ball outside the numbers, you stay outside those numbers.

No matter where the kickoff returner goes, the most embarrassing thing for him is to be tackled by the kicker. The kickoff returner has already run by ten guys trying to tackle him, and then the kicker tackles him. For a returner who's one of your fastest guys and an open-field runner, to be tackled by the kicker, that really hurts. His teammates will give him a lot of heat.

But for the kicker who makes the tackle, it's a great feeling. Jason Hanson of the Lions knows that feeling. After he made the tackle in a Thanksgiving Day game, he got up and strutted and spit. Making that tackle let him feel like one of the guys, like one of the real football players.

JIMMY JOHNSON COULDN'T LIVE WITHOUT IT

Coaches come and go, and come again. Sometimes when you don't expect it, like Bill Walsh rejoining the 49ers as an "administrative assistant," whatever that is. Or sometimes when you do expect it, like Jimmy Johnson being the Dolphins' coach now.

As soon as Don Shula decided to stop coaching the Dolphins, their owner, H. Wayne Huizenga, had to hire Jimmy and give him complete control of the football operation. Wayne couldn't go through one of those coaching carousels where he interviewed one guy one day, another guy the next day, a third guy the day after. You don't replace Don Shula with some assistant coach who deserves a chance to be a head coach. You hire the best coach available, especially if he's the best name. And you don't take long to do it.

"Wayne just threw me the keys like somebody throwing you the keys to their car," Jimmy told me. "When

I went in there to see Wayne the first day, I really wasn't sure I was going to take it, but he threw me the keys and said, 'Take over.'"

Jimmy was really enthused. We were in Dallas to do what would be his last pregame show for Fox at the NFC championship game, the day after he had signed a contract with the Dolphins, only a few hours after he had met with his new players. He was talking about Dan Marino and some of his other players, talking about which coaches to hire. Talking, talking, talking. He was so enthused, so excited, I got excited listening to him. Walking back to our hotel with Matt Millen that night, I was still excited.

"This is the first time since I got out of coaching that I ever envied a coach," I told Matt. "The first time I ever wished I was coaching again. It's the first time I've had that feeling. Hey, I just hope it goes away."

It did go away. Hey, I miss things about coaching. Being with my players, teaching them, developing them, getting ready for games on Sunday, especially the big games. That's what it was all about. Taking your team out there against the other team. I still have the games, but it's not the same. It'll never be the same, but I can live without it.

Jimmy Johnson couldn't live without it.

As soon as he took over the Dolphins, he showed that he still had a passion for coaching, that he hadn't had enough of it when he split with Jerry Jones early in 1994 after winning two Super Bowls with the Cowboys. Whenever I saw him at Fox meetings, he talked about how he wasn't sure if he would coach again, about how much he enjoyed not just television but having more time to spend in his home and yacht in the Florida Keys, more time to appreciate life.

"But if I ever coach again," he told me, "it would have to be on my terms."

To me, that meant the job had to be the perfect job, at least perfect for him. Here is a guy who loves south Florida not only because he coached the University of Miami's team to two national college championships, but also because he hates cold weather. Hates it. Jimmy Johnson never wants to have to buy an overcoat or gloves. But if you look at NFL cities on a map, most of them get cold late in the season. For him to come back, he needed more than a big multimillion-dollar contract. If it's just making money, there are a lot easier ways to do it. With his Fox and HBO television shows, he had one of those easier ways. So for him the perfect team had to be in Florida, preferably south Florida, but there's only one team in south Florida and that's the Dolphins and when Don Shula left, Jimmy's perfect job opened up.

By being so enthusiastic that night in Dallas, he also showed that he hadn't had enough of the drudgery of coaching. Not the games. They're the best part. I'm thinking of the long hours during the week, looking at film, worrying about players, preparing for the college draft, setting up your minicamps and training camp, going through the preseason. Those are the hardest things. Not the games.

In Dallas, the hardest thing for Jimmy was working with Jerry Jones. Not long after Troy Aikman signed his eight-year contract during the 1993 season, I remember talking to Troy about it.

"I signed this long-term contract based on what's here now," he told me. "I just hope things stay the same. I hope Norv Turner stays here, but I don't think he will. He'll probably be a head coach somewhere." Two months later Norv was named the Redskins' head coach. "I just hope," Troy added, "that Jimmy stays."

After the Cowboys practice that day, I mentioned that to Jimmy.

"Now that Troy has signed an eight-year contract," I said, "he's hoping you're here for those eight years."

"Are you kidding?" Jimmy said, laughing. "Eight years! No way."

"How about four?" I said.

"Four years or four months?"

I laughed. I thought he was kidding. Here was a coach on top of the world. He had so many good players. He was on his way to winning his second straight Super Bowl. But four months later, almost to the day, Jimmy was no longer the Cowboys' coach. Even when I remembered Jimmy saying, "Four years or four months?" I didn't put it together that he and Jerry would have what divorce lawyers call irreconcilable differences. One thing they had in common was that they could be whatever you wanted 'em to be, or be from wherever you wanted 'em to be from.

From Texas? Yeah, Jimmy was born in Galveston and Jerry had drilled for oil and gas there.

From Arkansas? Yeah, Jimmy and Jerry had played there together, even roomed there together.

From Oklahoma? Yeah, Jimmy had coached there and Jerry had drilled for oil and gas there.

But they weren't good friends. The only reason they roomed together at the University of Arkansas was that roommates were assigned alphabetically. They weren't best friends in college, they weren't best friends after college, and it turned out they certainly weren't best friends when they were together with the Cowboys, but whenever I talked to Jimmy or Jerry, neither one ever griped to me about the other.

The thing I really respected about them is that when they came into the NFL in 1989, both were criticized to the point of being laughed at because they had never been in the pro game. Jerry was a wildcat oil and gas guy. Jimmy was a college coach from the University of Miami, a rah-rah guy who ran long practices.

When the Cowboys went 1–15 their first year, they both stuck to their beliefs. Jerry talked as if the Cowboys had won the Super Bowl when they were the NFL's worst team. Jimmy had known enough to take Troy Aikman with the first pick in the 1989 draft, and he kept adding speed to the roster. I remember him saying, "I can't believe how slow this team is at every position. At Miami we had speed. We don't have any speed here." He used the draft choices he got from the Vikings in the Herschel Walker trade to get better players, like Emmitt Smith, Russell Maryland, Darren Woodson, Kevin Smith, and Clayton Holmes. He even hired an assistant coach, Bob Slowik, just to tutor his nickel backs. And the Cowboys started winning.

When the Cowboys won their two Super Bowls, I thought Jimmy was doing a good job as the coach and getting his share of the credit. I thought Jerry was doing a good job as the owner and getting his share of the credit.

There's an old saying in sports: "Winning is a great deodorant." Winning usually solves whatever problems exist. Winning usually stops whatever smells exist. Jerry and Jimmy proved that theory to be wrong. And their divorce created another theory: When a team wins consistently, there's not enough room for more than one ego. Here were two talented and successful guys with gigantic egos. Even with two Super Bowl rings, there wasn't enough credit to satisfy both of them, especially when Jerry told some writers, "There are five hundred coaches who could win with this team." That was the straw that broke Jimmy's back.

But no matter what happened in Dallas between them, I knew that sooner or later Jimmy would coach again. Because he's a football coach. That's what he does. He needed to coach again.

So did Bill Walsh. When the 49ers announced that he was coming back as an administrative assistant, he described himself as an "assistant coach." I was surprised that he would come back as an assistant anything, but the

49ers making that move didn't surprise me. Their owner, Eddie DeBartolo, is a real competitor, a real fighter with a lot of pride. When the 49ers got knocked out of the 1995 playoffs by the Packers, he wasn't going to stand pat. His hiring Bill Walsh was a reaction not just to losing that playoff game, but losing it to a team that was using the 49ers' offense better than the 49ers were using the 49ers' offense.

Mike Holmgren, the Packers' coach who had been Bill Walsh's offensive coordinator, had taken the 49ers' system, the so-called West Coast offense, to Green Bay, and developed Brett Favre into an All-Pro quarterback. The 49ers, meanwhile, had changed their offense to where their biggest goal was just to get the ball to Jerry Rice as often as they could.

The 49ers had gotten away from what was really Bill Walsh's system, so Eddie DeBartolo decided to bring back the coach that developed Joe Montana and the West Coast offense, the coach who won three Super Bowl games. But nobody seems to know exactly what Bill is coming back as, including him. I can't see Bill Walsh just being a consultant. To me, a consultant is somebody who comes in and goes out, somebody who makes suggestions but doesn't have much authority. If Bill says something, do the other coaches have to do it or not? Will his suggestions be suggestions, or will they be commands?

However it develops, George Seifert has said, "If we don't win, I'll be the one accountable." George's low-key personality might make it work. He says he had suggested bringing Bill back as offensive coordinator the year before, after Mike Shanahan left to be the Broncos' coach. George is the NFL's most underrated and underappreciated coach. All he does is win—two Super Bowl rings as the 49ers' head coach with a 95–30 record (including the postseason) and a 76 percent winning record, the best in NFL history. He also has three other Super Bowl rings as Bill Walsh's defensive coordinator.

Whatever happens, it will be interesting to have Bill Walsh and Jimmy Johnson in the mix with Barry Switzer. Even though the Cowboys won Super Bowl XXX with Barry as their coach, he's one of those guys that's a lightning rod for controversy. Whatever he does or doesn't do attracts attention, like the fourth-and-one situation in Philadelphia late in the 1995 season. I can't remember any one situation that had such a long shelf life before it died, but if the Cowboys don't keep winning, it will be resurrected.

You probably remember the situation: fourth down and one (really 1 foot, not 1 yard) at the Cowboys' 29-yard line with the score 17–17 and the clock winding down to the two-minute warning. But instead of the Cowboys' punt team coming onto the field, the offense lined up to go for a first down. It's one thing to go for it on fourth down in the other team's territory or even around midfield. It's another thing to go for it on your own 29-yard line in a tie game with two minutes left on the road. Up in the booth with Pat Summerall, I couldn't understand Barry's decision.

"Ooooh, I don't believe in this," I said. "I think tie score in this situation, unless they are going to try to draw them offsides, I think they cannot go for it here."

I don't like to second-guess a coach's decision. Anybody can do that. That's why I said what I did before the play was run. I had first-guessed it. I don't want to be quiet, then after they go for it and don't make it, say, "They should have punted." I want to say, Hey, this is wrong. You have to say it before, not after. If they get the first down, so be it. But when the Cowboys lined up to go for it, I couldn't just let it happen and then, if they don't get it, jump on it. I jumped on it before the snap, then Emmitt Smith took a hand-off from Troy Aikman, ran off left tackle, and the Eagles swarmed all over him. No gain, maybe even a 1-yard loss. Repeating my first guess, I said, "That's a bad call. You can't do that. That call could've won the Eagles this game."

"They're in field-goal range right now," Pat said.

"All they have to do is run that clock down," I said.

Now the commotion started over whether the clock had hit two minutes before the snap. If it does, the ball is dead. No play. On the sideline Barry Switzer was waving his hands.

"Barry is saying the two-minute warning," Pat said.

"Barry ought to be saying that he shouldn't have called that play," I said.

On our replay, it looked as if the snap just beat 2:00 on the clock. We couldn't tell if a whistle had been blown, but line judge Dave Anderson (a twelfth-year official who is an insurance executive in Salem, Oregon, not my collaborator on this book) seemed to be waving his hands a split second after the snap. Whatever happened, referee Ed Hochuli accepted the line judge's call.

"The two-minute warning occurred before the ball was snapped," Hochuli announced. "Therefore, it's fourth down."

But instead of sending out the punting team on fourth down this time, Barry Switzer kept the Cowboy offense on the field.

"I'm surprised the Cowboys are going for it again," I said. "I think that was a bad call the first time they did it. I think it's a bad call now."

Emmitt Smith took a hand-off again, ran off left tackle again, and was stopped again.

"Didn't get it again," I said. "That's unbelievable. This is unbelievable. What in the heck is going on? The score is tied. You're on the road. Whoooo, I don't know." When the replay came up, I said, "There's no place here. I mean, this is short-yardage defense. The Eagles are selling out against the run. They have everyone up. They just read the thing. There's no chance. There's no chance to get that ball in there against that defense."

"The linebackers come fill the hole," Pat said. "The defensive backs are in the hole."

"The line controlled the line of scrimmage," I said. "But still, even that call, when you're in that area of the field, you have to punt the ball."

When another replay seemed to show that the line judge started waving his hands a split second after the snap, I said, "I thought they dodged a bullet, they'd go back and punt. They did the same thing. They deserve to lose."

They did lose, 20–17, when Gary Anderson kicked a 42-yard field goal.

For the next few days, if not for the next few weeks until the Cowboys won Super Bowl XXX, just about everybody kicked Barry Switzer around. His explanation for going for the first down was that on ten previous fourth-and-a-foot situations, the Cowboys had gone for it and made it all ten times. He also mentioned that had the Cowboys punted into the wind, the Eagles would have had time to move into position for the winning field goal, which some people interpreted as a slap at his defense.

Back when I was coaching the Raiders, whenever we had a fourth-and-one situation, my players would always be yelling, "We can make it, we can make it." The more they yelled, the more I told them, "If you can make it, you would've made it on third down."

In the Cowboys' situation, they went for it on fourth down, which is not a good percentage play, and they didn't make it. After the referee waved that play off, they went for it again, after they had proved they couldn't make it in that situation in that position on the field against that team on that day in that stadium. As for having to punt into the wind, even with a 30-yard punt, the Eagles would have had to go 30 yards to get back to the Cowboys' 29-yard line. By not punting and not making it, the Cowboys put the Eagles into instant field-goal position. All the Eagles had to do was run a few plays to take some time off the clock, then kick the field goal. That's exactly what happened.

When the Cowboys not only lost that game but also lost the home-field advantage through the NFC playoffs (which they later regained when the 49ers lost their season finale in Atlanta), Barry's decision became the story of that game. The only story.

As a result, some things were forgotten. Like how well the Eagles played, especially in the second half when they shut down Emmitt Smith, shut off Troy Aikman, and shut out Michael Irvin. Also forgotten was how Barry had to take all the heat, and how well he took it. When he heard about the *New York Post*'s back-page headline that shouted, "Bozo the Coach," he laughed. He even asked for a copy of it.

"I want to show it to my kids," he said.

When I saw him in Dallas later that week, before the Cowboys were to play the Giants, he had to know that I had first-guessed his decision. But he never brought it up. I didn't either. Not a word. To both of us, it was over and done with, let's talk about the next game. Maybe that was because he's a coach and I used to be a coach. I knew what he was going through. I'm a firm believer that when a team wins, you should give the credit to the same people that you give the blame to when the team loses. Whenever the Cowboys won, it was always Emmitt Smith and Troy Aikman and Michael Irvin and the offensive line and Deion Sanders and Charles Haley and offensive coordinator Ernie Zampese and defensive coordinator Dave Campo and special-teams coach Joe Avezzano.

Whenever the Cowboys lost, it was always Barry Switzer. The argument in that Eagle game is that the fourth and one was Barry's decision. But when you're the head coach, isn't everything your decision?

Isn't it Barry's decision when Troy Aikman throws a touchdown to Michael Irvin? Isn't it his decision when Deion Sanders returns a punt to set up a touchdown? Isn't it his decision when Emmitt Smith rushes for 150 yards and scores two touchdowns? Isn't that what the head coach's job is? Isn't he ultimately responsible for all the plays, all the defenses, all the decisions? Isn't he the one who decides when to take a time-out, when you accept penalties, when you decline penalties? Isn't he the one who manages the game?

When the Cowboys bounced back and beat the Steelers, 27–17, in Super Bowl XXX, nobody brought up Barry Switzer's decision to go for it on the fourth and one in Philadelphia six weeks earlier. But if the Cowboys hadn't won that Super Bowl, he would've gotten as much heat, if not more, than Don Shula did in Miami.

When I started out as a young coach in college, the coach I always studied and respected and watched and wanted to be like was Vince Lombardi, but when I got into pro football, Don Shula was the coach I respected the most. As a head coach in the NFL, there's not a lot of other coaches to talk to, to run things by. When you're a high-school coach, you can talk to other high-school coaches. When you're a college coach, you can talk to other college coaches. But when you're an NFL coach, there aren't a lot of other NFL coaches you can talk to. Most of them don't want to talk to you. It's too competitive. But there were two coaches I could always talk to and did talk to, about coaching and trends and handling players and minicamps and training camp and workout schedules. One was Don Shula, the other was George Allen, who was coaching the Redskins then.

With George Allen, the conversations were always about the other team. George was defensively oriented so anytime the Redskins had an AFC team coming up, he'd ask me, "Who's the number one guy I have to take away? Who's the number two guy?" Anytime we were playing an NFC team, he'd want the Raiders to beat them, so he would tell me anything he thought might help.

But with Don Shula, the conversations were about the philosophy of coaching, things like trends and handling players and minicamps and training camp and workout schedules. One year I read that the Dolphins were having walk-through workouts. At the time I had never heard of a walk-through workout, so I called him to find out what it was.

"John," he said, "it's just a meeting on the field."

In a meeting room you can diagram the play, you can show film of the play, but you can't walk through the play. Out on the practice field, you can line up the players and you can walk through the play. It's a great way to teach.

Just another reason why back when I was the Raiders' coach and through all my years in broadcasting, whenever somebody asked me who was the best NFL coach, I always said, "Don Shula."

He won more NFL games (328 in the regular season and 347 counting the postseason, including Super Bowls VII and VIII) and he did it over more than three decades in different eras with different teams, different players, and different staffs.

"How do you do it?" I once asked him.

"I don't let things bother me that I can't control," he said.

"I could never do that," I said.

Maybe that's why I lasted only ten years as the Raiders' coach. Don lasted thirty-three years, seven with the Baltimore Colts and twenty-six with the Dolphins. I let little things bother me. I think most coaches do. Don didn't. Not even when his quarterback got hurt. When Dan Marino needed Achilles tendon surgery in 1994, Don put in Scott Mitchell and kept winning. When Bob Griese had a broken ankle early in the 1972 season, he put in Earl Morrall and not only kept winning but, with Griese returning in the AFC championship game and Super Bowl VII, had a 17–0 season. When Johnny Unitas hurt his ribs in 1968, he put in Morrall and the Colts won the NFL title before losing Super Bowl III to the Jets. And when he didn't have Marino or Griese or Unitas, he took the 1982 Dolphins to the Super Bowl with a quarterback not many people remember, David Woodley.

But the longer you stay in coaching, the tougher the defeats are, the less enjoyable the wins are. I found that as a young coach, you really enjoy the wins and you get down on the losses too, but as you get older, you don't enjoy the wins as much.

I remember talking to Joe Gibbs during his last season as the Redskins' coach. Here's a guy with three Super Bowl rings telling me, "The longer you coach, the wins don't seem to be as big but the losses are much bigger." Maybe after you win it all, you're harder to satisfy.

Even if you win the Super Bowl, you don't get any time to enjoy it anymore because someone that night will ask you, "Can you repeat?" Now they've got that new word. *Three-peat.* If you win the Super Bowl, somebody might even ask, "Can you repeat and maybe three-peat?" Hey, we haven't even *re*peated.

In his last season, Don Shula's team had a 9–7 record and made the playoffs. For most teams, that's a good year. But when your name is Don Shula, it's not enough for you or the fans.

There has to be an end to everything. No player goes on playing forever. No coach goes on coaching forever. No owner goes on owning forever. Everything comes to an end. So you knew there had to be an end even for Don Shula, but he deserved a classier way for it to end. He took too much ridicule in Miami his last few seasons. He had been the best coach. He stood for everything that was good about football, everything that was good about being a coach, everything that was good about being a man. I hated to see him stripped of all that. But his last few seasons, it seemed like too many people in Miami forgot what he once did.

Don was always a teacher who believed in organization and discipline. I'm sure he got that from Paul Brown when he was a defensive back with the Cleveland Browns. I think Don might have got his devotion to duty at an advanced age from Paul Brown too.

Except for the few Raiders games I coached against Paul Brown when he was with the Bengals, I hardly knew him, but everyone who had ever been around him as a player or as an assistant coach raved about what a brilliant coach he was. Two of his Browns players, Don Shula and Chuck Noll, turned out to be two of the NFL's greatest coaches. All the elements of today's pro football, Paul Brown created them in Cleveland—assistant coaches, playbooks, meeting rooms, film study, putting the players in a hotel the night before a game, calling plays from the sideline and sending it in with a messenger guard (Chuck Noll was one of those messenger guards).

At the time most people thought, "He must be some kind of nut. The quarterback should be calling the plays." Now coaches send in just about every play. And that thing in the quarterbacks' helmets now where they hear the play being called from the sideline, Paul Brown had one of those in quarterback George Ratterman's helmet almost half a century ago.

Don Shula had seen Paul Brown go on to coach the Bengals until he was sixty-seven and remain as their president and general manager until his death in 1991. When the 1988 Bengals got to the Super Bowl, Paul Brown was a lively eighty. Hey, if Paul Brown stayed on the job that long, Don wanted to stay on the job that long. The ironic thing about people in Miami saying that at nearly sixty-six Don was too old to coach and that the game had passed him by was that (in what turned out to be Don's career finale) the Dolphins lost a wild-card playoff in Buffalo to the Bills whose coach, Marv Levy, was seventy at the time. According to the Bills' media guide, Marv was only sixty-seven, but when he confessed to really being seventy, nobody was saying he's too old. During that 1995 season he had surgery for prostate cancer but after missing three games, he was back on the sideline in Buffalo.

Even though the Bills lost a divisional playoff in Pittsburgh, in winning the AFC East and beating the Dolphins in a wild-card playoff, they had done more than most people expected. Nobody cared if Marv was seventy or seven hundred.

In Miami, the expectations were greater. Nobody had complained about Don's age when the Dolphins got off to a 4–0 start with a team that many people thought would get to Super Bowl XXX as the AFC champion. But when the Dolphins started to struggle, the critics got all over him. That's normal, but I thought Don's record had put him above all that. Maybe that's being idealistic. Maybe no matter how long you've coached, no matter how many games you've won, no matter how classy you've been, if you don't win, there's no deodorant strong enough to stop the smell.

Marv Levy reminds me of George Allen. The same intensity, the same attention to detail, even the same way of talking and the same mannerisms. Maybe he picked all that up when he was George's special-teams coach on the Redskins.

If George had lived, he would've wanted to coach forever too. Most of the good ones do, like Bill Parcells. When he quit the Giants in 1991 after winning two Super Bowls, his health was one of the reasons. His heart was beating faster than it was supposed to. He had the operation where they put a balloon in an artery, then he had another balloon, then he had a bypass operation. I thought, "Enough, you've got your two Super Bowls," but when he took the Patriots job, I called and asked him why.

"I don't know," he told me.

"But after all your heart stuff, why did you do it?"

"You know me. I just did it."

I started to laugh. This was the same Bill Parcells that I knew when he was the Giants' coach. Always fun to talk to, always one jump ahead of everybody.

"I've got a deal for you," he said. "Come to training camp and coach with me. I'll give you the linebackers. Just hang out with me for two weeks at training camp."

He had me laughing again, but now we got serious.

"Did you get an option to buy the franchise?" I asked. "You know the ownership there is up in the air. If you got an option to buy, if anything happened, you could put together your own group of money guys and be part of the ownership."

"No," he said. "I was more interested in the long-term contracts I got for my assistant coaches."

That tells you a lot about Bill Parcells. Some head coaches will take care of their own contracts, but they won't fight for their assistants' contracts. Bill does. He knows that an assistant's job security depends on the head coach. He grew up as an assistant on several college staffs. He was an assistant with the Patriots and the Giants before he became a head coach.

Most of the Super Bowl–winning head coaches were assistants on NFL staffs—Vince Lombardi, Don Shula, Chuck Noll, Bill Walsh, Joe Gibbs, Tom Landry, Bill Parcells, George Seifert, Tom Flores, Mike Ditka, Weeb Ewbank, Don McCafferty. Hey, even me.

I think it's important to have been an NFL assistant coach. It's part of paying your dues, putting in your time. Sometimes you can just tell from the way an assistant talks and thinks that someday he'll be a good head coach, like when Dan Reeves was one of Tom Landry's assistants on the Cowboys. In 1978, what turned out to be my last year as the Raiders' coach, the NFL increased the regular season to sixteen games and shortened the preseason schedule from six games to four. To get a better look at our rookies that year, we arranged to practice and scrimmage against the Cowboys at their training camp in Thousand Oaks, California. At lunch one day, I was talking to Dan.

"We need more toughness," he said.

"You mean in your running backs?" I asked, knowing those were the players he was in charge of.

"No, the whole team," he said.

I liked that. Dan wasn't second-guessing Tom Landry, he was just talking like a head coach, thinking like a head coach. Another assistant coach might say, "I just coach the running backs," but he was thinking about the entire team. Even though the Cowboys had won the Super Bowl the previous season, he knew that to win it again they needed more toughness to go with their finesse. He knew because he had been a tough running back himself in short-yardage and goal-line situations. He knew how important that toughness was. When he became the Broncos' head coach in 1981, he incorporated the Cowboys' finesse with toughness and when he moved to the Giants in 1993, he did the same thing.

Dan knows how to play the game. His first year with the Giants, he didn't have enough good players to be dominant on offense or defense, so he strengthened his kicking game. He got three guys he had in Denver to help get good field position—Brad Daluiso to kick off, Mike Horan to punt to the sidelines, and David Treadwell to kick field goals.

Daluiso kicked off into the end zone, so the other team was always starting on its 20-yard line, with 80 yards to go. Horan punted out of bounds, which took away a good return. When the Giants got the ball back, they didn't have to go far for Treadwell to kick a field goal. That's coaching. That's doing the little things that a team needs to win when it's not dominant on offense or defense. The Giants were 11–5 that year and won a wild-card playoff.

I don't get to see the AFC coaches as much because Fox does mostly NFC games, but I like the job Bill Cowher has done with the Steelers.

As soon as Bill got the job in 1992, he worked hard and got his kind of players. At first he did it with defense and special teams, then he got a running game going, then he got the most out of quarterback Neil O'Donnell, who is with the Jets now, by using four and five wide receivers. And in Kordell Stewart, he may have started something that other coaches will do. Two quarterbacks in the huddle.

Stewart's nickname is Slash, as in quarterback/wide receiver. But he's basically a quarterback.

Whenever both Stewart and O'Donnell were in the huddle, when they came out, one was the quarterback and the other was a wide receiver. But when the other team has to call its defense, it doesn't know which one is going to be the quarterback. To do this, one of the quarterbacks has to be a good wide receiver, which is what Stewart gave them. O'Donnell didn't scare the other team as a wide receiver. But two quarterbacks coming out of the huddle is something other coaches may go to. Ray Rhodes, the Eagles' coach, even talked about doing it with Rodney Peete and Randall Cunningham.

"You mean alternating your quarterbacks?" Ray was asked.

"No," he said, "I mean playing both at the same time."

Ray Rhodes is a good coach, a good motivator, a good judge of talent. He really knows the defensive side, so he understands how two quarterbacks would confuse the other team's defense. But to use two quarterbacks effectively, you need one who's a threat as a wide receiver. Now that Kordell Stewart has done it, other coaches might start looking for a quarterback who can also be a threat as a wide receiver. Cowher also started something else, the zone blitz on defense that drops defensive linemen into zone coverages while linebackers blitz.

Dom Capers, who had been the Steelers' defensive coordinator, took that zone blitz to Carolina as the Cougars' head coach. You don't need the best defensive players and the best pass rushers because by changing up, the other team doesn't know which one is coming.

Marty Schottenheimer is another coach who's always coming up with new schemes. The day before the 49ers played in Kansas City in 1994, I was sitting in his office asking him about the Chiefs and every so often he would refer to this big thick binder that he had on his desk.

"What is that?" I finally asked.

"That's the game plan. That's all the week's work. That's everything we've done preparing for the 49ers."

Then he picked it up and tossed it to me.

"Here," he said. "Take a look at it."

The day before a game, some coaches are paranoid. They know I'm not going to steal their game plan, but they don't talk about it much. And no coach ever let me look at his game plan before. But that day Marty had so much confidence in what he was doing, he just tossed that big thick binder to me and let me look at it. But all I really did was look at the size of it, at all the detail. I put together the Raiders' game plans, and I've seen what other teams' game plans look like, but this one had ten times more stuff than I'd ever seen.

"Do the players get all this?" I asked.

"No, some is just for my coaches and me," he said. "Tendencies, breakdowns, stuff like that."

The next day the Chiefs upset the 49ers.

Of all the NFL coaches, I think the Saints' Jim Mora is the one who has done the most with the least. He's never had what you would call a great team or a great quarter-back, and the Saints had to play the 49ers twice every season, but they always played the 49ers tough. Whether the quarterback was Joe Montana or Steve Young, the 49ers made a living on first and second downs hitting short passes to the tight end or the running back in that area 3 yards beyond the line of scrimmage, because the other team's linebackers were always dropping into an area 10 to 12 yards deep. In the history of defense, that shallow area between the pass-rushing linemen and the linebackers was always open until Jim Mora zoned that area. After that, the 49ers couldn't throw it to that area because the Saints had taken it away. Jim Mora was the first to do that, then other teams did it.

One of the most interesting things in coaching is how the 49ers turn on a video camera in their meeting room whenever their offensive coordinator puts in a play in training camp. The video shows how the coach introduces the play, how he diagrams it, how he explains it.

Bill Walsh started that videotape library when he put in plays as the 49ers' head coach. When he hired Mike Holmgren in 1986 as quarterback coach, Mike studied those tapes.

"I had thirty big tapes," Mike told me. "This is how I learned the 49ers' offense. I watched how Bill installed at training camp what added up to thousands of plays."

Now, a decade later, the 49ers have thousands more. When Mike Holmgren was promoted to offensive coordi-nator in 1989, he was videotaped putting in the plays. When he left to be the Packers' coach in 1992 (and started his own library by having himself videotaped putting in the Packers' plays), his successor as the 49ers' coordinator, Mike Shanahan, was videotaped putting in the plays. Then when Mike Shanahan left to be the Broncos' coach in 1995, his successor as coordinator, Marc Trestman, was videotaped putting in the plays.

Another team can copy a 49ers playoff game film, but it doesn't know exactly how Bill Walsh or any of the offensive coordinators explained it. Another team doesn't know the 49ers' coaching points. Every play has coaching points, like the different patterns the pass receivers would run against different defenses.

To the 49ers, the real value was that any of their coordinators could go back and see how his predecessors had put in a certain play, or how Bill Walsh himself had put in a certain play.

And when Bill returned to the 49ers in 1996 as an administrative assistant, whatever that is, he could even go back and see how he had put in a certain play. Not that he needed to. Coaches come and go and come again, but they never forget a play.

HATING THE COWBOYS IS HEALTHY

When I'm not doing the Super Bowl, I'm like everybody else. I watch it on television with some friends. But watching Super Bowl XXX, I couldn't understand why most of my friends were rooting for the Steelers. These were people who live in northern California, people who are 49ers fans. No way they would be rooting for the Steelers. They couldn't name five players on the Steelers.

Then I realized, hey, they weren't rooting for the Steelers, they were rooting against the Cowboys.

Once upon a time the Cowboys were known as America's Team. No matter where you lived, if you didn't have a team there or you didn't particularly like any team, you rooted for the Cowboys. Their nickname was enough. Everybody likes cowboys. For years, the Cowboys really were America's Team, especially when Roger Staubach was their quarterback and Tom Landry was their coach.

Now the Cowboys are Jerry Jones's team, but not everybody likes that. Ever since he bought the Cowboys in 1989, some of his moves have changed their image. His split with Jimmy Johnson. His multimillion-dollar deals with Nike, Pepsi-Cola, and American Express. His signing Deion Sanders for $35 million. His sideline smiles for the cameras. He's created a new breed of Cowboy haters.

Instead of always being lovable cowpokes, these Cowboys now are considered by some people to be the baddest kind in the old West—cattle rustlers.

To me, that love-hate relationship is healthy for pro football but I don't know if the NFL would agree. Some owners resented how Jerry Jones circumvented the $37.1 million salary cap by paying $62 million in salaries and bonuses during the 1995 season. The NFL sued him for $300 million for making his marketing deals in defiance of NFL Properties, then he countersued for $750 million. And when somebody asked him how many of the other twenty-nine owners he thought were rooting for him and the Cowboys in the 1995 NFC championship game, he had to stop and think for a few seconds.

"About six and a half," he finally said.

That love-hate relationship means that people care what happens to the Cowboys now, good or bad. Love 'em, like some people do. Hate 'em, like my friends did watching Super Bowl XXX. Whichever it is, people care with feeling, with passion. That's important. But only a dominant team can create that feeling. Some people think that parity is good for the NFL, but I don't. All those 8–6 and 7–7 and 6–9 teams late in the season are just mediocre teams that don't inspire much feeling or much passion the way a dominant team does.

Years ago it was that way in baseball when the Yankees won the World Series so often. When they had Babe Ruth, Lou Gehrig, Joe DiMaggio, and Mickey Mantle, they were so good for so long, as many people hated them as loved them.

It was that way in boxing with Muhammad Ali. Some people hated his big mouth, but after his three-and-a-half-year exile for refusing to go into the military service, other people loved him for sticking to his beliefs, then for winning back the title from George Foreman and for retaining it in the Thrilla in Manila with Joe Frazier.

It was that way in pro football with the Jets' Joe Namath and his playboy image, his long hair. Some people loved him, others hated him. It was that way with the Raiders. I know. I was their coach then. Nobody was neutral about the Raiders. You either loved them and wanted them to win. Or you hated them and wanted them to lose.

It's been that way in wrestling ever since Gorgeous George and the other heroes and villains split the crowd.

Now it's that way with the Cowboys. Jerry Jones knew his team would only be as good as its best players (Emmitt Smith, Troy Aikman, Michael Irvin, Charles Haley, Deion Sanders), so he made sure to sign them with the money he got from marketing his product, even his stadium.

Traditionalists resent that because traditionalists are always looking back to what was. Jerry is always looking ahead to what will be. Whenever I go to Dallas to do a Cowboys game, I like to talk to him, listen to him, watch him.

The Thursday before the NFC championship game with the Packers he picked up my son Mike and me at our hotel to show us this tract of land outside Dallas he plans to develop. He had to stop for gas so he pulled into a self-service station. He's out there pumping his own gas when the guy in the car in front of us recognized him.

"Jerry Jones," the guy said, "I just want to shake your hand and get your autograph."

As they shook hands, the phone in Jerry's car rang. He handed the gas handle to the guy, jumped in the car, and answered the phone. While he talked, the guy was pumping Jerry's gas. He finally hung up, hopped out of the car, signed the autograph, shook hands again, put the cap on the tank, paid for his gas, and we drove off. Except he was talking so much about his land, he forgot which way to go. We were lost for half an hour. He had to call his secretary, Marylyn Love, to have her look at a map and tell him where he was and how to get where we were going.

That's Jerry Jones. His real sport is business. He wants to win in business, whether that business is the Cowboys, oil and gas, land development, whatever.

Instead of fighting him, the other NFL club owners should try to learn from him how to market pro football. Build up stars. Promote the teams. Brighten the stadiums. Instead of worrying so much about what Jerry is doing, the owners should be meeting about how to make the game better for fans, how to make officiating better, how to make the preseason better.

The preseason is the NFL's primary promotion but more and more, coaches and players talk about having too many preseason games, about the best players not playing because they don't want to get hurt. Maybe there should be fewer preseason games. Maybe there should be none.

In the owners' meetings, all they ever talk about is the salary cap and free agency, or how to stop a team from moving to another city, or whatever Jerry Jones has done lately. Like using Texas Stadium to market the Cowboys not only as a pro football team but as a business.

Quarterbacks and other stars get paid for wearing a certain brand of shoe, for wearing the latest cap on the sideline. Coaches get paid for wearing the latest sweater or jacket or parka. Any signage that players or coaches wear, they get paid for. That's been going on for years. One NFL coach's contract once included a clause giving him the marketing rights to his sideline, then he sold the rights back to the club.

Jerry Jones just extended that idea. If a player's shoes or hats were worth so much, if a coach's sweater and jacket were worth so much, he figured that Texas Stadium had to be worth something. He made a deal to put a Nike swoosh on it.

Once upon a time the only thing that mattered in a football stadium was how many seats. The edifice itself didn't mean much. Now the edifice is the thing. But for any edifice to be a marketing monument, it has to be state of the art. The more luxury boxes, the better. The fancier, the better. Jerry's plan to increase the seating capacity of Texas Stadium from 65,812 to about 100,000 is only the beginning. He wants to create a theme-park atmosphere around Texas Stadium with a Cowboy Hall of Fame, video presentations and interactive computer games, a hotel and restaurants, a Cowboyland that fans will want to visit not just when there's a Cowboys game but during the week and in the off-season.

Jerry Jones wants to do what Las Vegas did in stealing customers from Disneyland.

During one of our off-season Fox meetings in 1994, our hotel was in Anaheim because the World Cup soccer tournament had filled all the Los Angeles hotels. But years ago the Anaheim hotels were always packed in the summer with families going to Disneyland. One day I asked the bellman what happened.

"Las Vegas," he said.

I knew what he meant. For years the casinos in Las Vegas were the attraction, but only adults went there. Now the new hotels had their casinos, but they were also theme parks that attracted the whole family. The Mirage had white tigers behind a long glass window, dolphins in a huge pool, a rain forest in the lobby, exotic fish in a tank behind the registration desk. The MGM Grand had a movie lot. The message to the adults was, Hey, bring your kids, look at the animals, watch how movies are made.

That's what Jerry Jones wants to do with his Cowboyland theme park. Bring your kids, visit the Hall of Fame, look at the videos, do the interactive stuff, stay at the hotel, go to the restaurants.

New state-of-the-art stadiums will differentiate pro football from college football. Notre Dame can't threaten to move to California or Florida if South Bend, Indiana, doesn't build it a new stadium. Notre Dame is in South Bend to stay. If it wants a new stadium, Notre Dame has to pay for it. So it fixes up its old stadium every so often. For five or six games a year, a fixed-up old stadium is all you need in college football. But in pro football, a new state-of-the-art stadium in another city is a temptation some owners can't resist.

Art Modell couldn't resist. That's why Baltimore now has Modell's team, nicknamed the Ravens, while Cleveland has to wait until no later than 1999 for a new team.

Modell moving his team was franchise free agency. Every time a player moves as a free agent, you can't always blame him for leaving or blame the club for letting him go. Sometimes it's the player's decision. Sometimes it's management's decision. Sometimes it's just the system. When you take that a step further, when a franchise is free from its stadium commitment, that ups its value, like the $50 million upfront bonus that Modell got to go to Baltimore. Maybe someday that bonus will be $100 million for another team in another city.

Even if a team got free stadium rent for thirty years in the city where it is, I don't think it's going to get a big bonus to stay there. But to keep teams, maybe cities will need to do that.

Hey, when the NFL agreed to put a team in Cleveland by 1999, it agreed to borrow anywhere from $28 million to $48 million (which the owner of the new Cleveland club would pay back with interest) to help finance a new seventy-two-thousand-seat, natural-grass, state-of-the-art stadium, either for an expansion team or a relocated team. Modell also agreed to pay Cleveland $11.5 million for lost rent, admissions, and property taxes.

The new Cleveland team will be known as the Browns,

and its uniforms will still be seal brown and orange, but it will never be quite the same for all those fans who rooted for Otto Graham, Jim Brown, Leroy Kelly, and Bernie Kosar.

Even though the Browns never went to a Super Bowl, most years seventy thousand of their fans showed up in Cleveland Stadium for every game. That's loyalty, but when Modell left for Baltimore, he showed that it's hard to be loyal in pro football now. The system doesn't always let you be loyal. When a player's contract expires, he's free to go and the club is free to let him go. When a club's stadium lease expires (or is about to expire), the franchise is free to go, to take the best offer from whatever city out there will come up with enough millions.

Most of this franchise movement is just pro football recycling. Except for the Oilers' move to Nashville by 1998, the teams involved have jumped to cities that had lost teams—the Browns to Baltimore, the Rams to St. Louis, the Raiders back to Oakland.

But that doesn't help the fans in Cleveland, Anaheim, Los Angeles, and Houston that rooted for those teams. When Al Davis won his antitrust case to take the Raiders to Los Angeles from Oakland before the 1982 season, it was real tough on the people of Oakland. Hey, it was tough on me even though I wasn't coaching the Raiders anymore. I live in the Oakland area, the East Bay area. I had coached the Raiders for ten seasons. The fans were great. Every game was a sellout. Suddenly the fans didn't have a team, but some never admitted that the Raiders had left. Some even went to Los Angeles to see Raiders games. And like me, most fans could never say "Los Angeles Raiders." They kept saying "Oakland Raiders." On the air, so I wouldn't mess it up, I just said "Raiders."

When the NFL talked about expansion, it was everywhere but Oakland. I always thought the only way Oakland would get a team was if the Raiders returned.

So when I read about the NFL either building a new

stadium in L.A. or the Raiders coming back in 1995, I knew this was Oakland's last chance. Once the Raiders agreed to a new stadium in L.A., then Oakland would never get another team. But the Raiders never got entrenched in the L.A. area. They never got their luxury boxes; and after the Northridge earthquake early in 1994, the L.A. Coliseum needed to be fixed. On my KNBR radio show one morning, I talked about how Oakland was never going to get as close to getting the Raiders back as it was right now, that this was like the tenth round of a twelve-round fight. Oakland couldn't stop fighting now. It had already fought ten rounds. It had to fight the last two rounds. Ed De Silva, the Oakland Coliseum board member who was negotiating with Al, must have heard me because he said, "We're going to fight the last two rounds." Not too long after that, Al called me.

"If we come back," he asked, "are there enough fans?"

"There's a lot more than when you left," I told him.

"But," he wanted to know, "can we sell enough tickets?"

I started to say that I didn't know about that, but then I said, "Hell, yes."

Al didn't say anything to that. He was still deciding.

The morning of June 21, when Frank Dill asked me on my KNBR radio show, "Heard anything about the Raiders lately?" I recalled how I had said a week earlier that they were closer to coming back than they ever had been since they left, and then I said, "Now they're closer than that. Everyone is saying, 'When is it going to come?' I think it's here now."

To me it was no longer the tenth round of a twelve-round fight. Now it was like the last ten seconds of the twelfth round.

"Having been an East Bay person and in Oakland and a Raider," I said, "I just feel so passionately about this, I just hope that it's going to come to pass. We've been talking about it a long time. It's a tough decision. It's not an easy decision. I know the support's here. I know that this is what it's all about. I've felt the Raiders belong here. I just hope there's about ten seconds left and I just hope everyone keeps swinging because I think we're as close as we've ever been and I think it's going to be done today."

Two days later, June 23, Al Davis signed a letter of intent to bring the Raiders back. I felt good. Oakland finally got a win. At the time not only were the baseball A's up for sale but there was talk of the franchise leaving the Oakland area, and the basketball Warriors were looking in San Francisco and San Jose at new arena sites. Once the Raiders returned, Oakland seemed to settle down. The A's were sold to new owners who promised to keep the franchise in Oakland and the Warriors eventually negotiated a new Coliseum deal.

Having lived through the Oakland situation, I understood what the fans in Cleveland went through, what the fans in other cities go through when their team leaves. Players come and go anyway. Coaches come and go anyway. Owners come and go anyway. But the fans don't. The fans live there and work there. But suddenly there's no team for them to be fans of.

Some club owners feel a little guilty about that. After Art Modell announced that he was taking his team out of Cleveland, he never went back there. He probably never will. After Al Davis took the Raiders to Los Angeles, he kept his home in the hills above Oakland, but whenever he returned from Los Angeles, he took a flight that landed at the San Francisco International Airport, then he rode over the Bay Bridge to his home. After the Raiders returned to Oakland in 1995, he did too.

"Now that we're back in Oakland," Al told me, "I can go in and out of the Oakland airport again."

WHY I COULDN'T COACH NOW

I've been out of coaching since 1978 and I have no desire to coach again, but as a broadcaster I've tried to keep thinking like a coach. Whatever has happened in the NFL, the turnover of players, the new rules, the new offenses and new defenses, the coordinators calling plays and defenses, the electronic device in the quarterback's helmet, whatever it's been, for a long time it really wasn't that much different from when I was coaching the Raiders. You get as many good players as you can, you coach 'em, and you play on Sunday.

But when the NFL put a salary cap on a team's payroll in 1994, for the first time I knew I couldn't coach now even if I wanted to.

With the salary cap, you can't get as many good players and you can't always keep your best players. You've heard the same line from every team, the one that goes, "We'd like to keep him but he's making so much money we have to let him leave as a free agent and get somebody else we can fit under the cap." I couldn't do that.

But if you're an NFL coach now, you've got to be willing to do that with a salary cap that was $40.7 million for each team in 1996, up from $37.1 million in 1995 and $34.6 million in 1994.

Building an NFL team is no longer based on putting together your best players, period. It's based now on putting together your best players whose salaries you can fit under the cap.

For a coach, a cap should be something you wear at practice along with a whistle around your neck while you hold a clipboard with your plays; a cap shouldn't be another word for budget.

As a coach, I was always big on loyalty. Both ways. The player to the team, the team to the player. That's where the salary cap hurts. It's easy for fans to say, "That player just walked away, he should've shown some loyalty to his team." But a team can't be loyal to a player either. You shouldn't tell a guy to play hard, we're all in this together, then tell him his salary is too high.

Look what happened to Phil Simms. He had a great year in 1993, but when the Giants couldn't fit his $2 million contract under the cap the next year, they released him.

With the players, there's not much *we* anymore. It's all *I* and *me* now. If club owners and general managers started evaluating and paying a player on the *we*, in other words how did we as a team do, maybe there would be more we players. But players are paid by the *I*, they're paid by their stats. That's what creates the problem. It's easy to say the players ought to think we, but they don't get paid by we, they get paid by I, so the players think I.

I don't blame players for trying to get all the money they can because they don't have much time to get it.

Some players will last ten or twelve or fifteen years, but most don't last anywhere near that. Even a high draft choice might not have that many opportunities to sign a

big contract. As a rookie, he'll sign, say, a four-year contract for good money. So now, in his fifth year, he'll have
one more window at a big contract, one more shot. That's
what it's all about now. He had his first shot as a rookie
and now, in his fifth year, this might be his last shot. So if
he's getting that last shot, he's got to make it a good one.
That's the reality of it now.

If everything were equal, maybe the player would
rather stay with his old team. But the system doesn't let
him.

That's what happened with Ricky Watters. Since he
was a restricted free agent, the 49ers had the right to
match whatever signed offer he got from another team. So
he was forced to go get an offer. When he got a three-year
$6.9 million deal from the Eagles, the 49ers had a week to
match it. When they chose not to match it, he belonged to
the Eagles.

The way the system works, when Ricky had a window
to get a big contract, he had to look out that window for
an offer. It couldn't be a bluff. He couldn't tell the 49ers,
"Hey, I was just kidding." The system locked him into
taking the Eagles' offer.

Sometimes the system works the other way around.
When another restricted free agent, Rodney Hampton, got
a signed six-year $16.5 million offer from the 49ers after
the 1995 season, he talked about what "an honor" it would
be to play with Jerry Rice and Steve Young, about how
opposing teams could no longer put up an eight-man
front to stop him. Standing there in his All-Madden sweatshirt at the 49ers complex, he sounded like he didn't want
to be a Giant anymore. But when the Giants matched the
offer, he said, "They really wanted me back, and I'm happy
to be back." But I wondered if he wouldn't have been even
happier with the 49ers.

Some people argue that the NFL is like college football
now with its turnover of players every year, but it's not. In

college you know you're getting new players every year, but when your players leave, you don't have to play against them.

In the years when Kenny Stabler was my quarterback on the Raiders, if he had walked away as a free agent to another team, it would've been hard for me to coach against him. Some people say, "What's the difference between a player changing teams in a trade or as a free agent?" There's a big difference. Even now the best NFL players are seldom traded. Maybe near the end of their career, but almost never when they are at their best.

You used to turn on a television set and you'd see Reggie White in a green uniform and you'd say, "Oh, the Eagles are playing." Or you'd see Joe Montana in a red uniform under the center and you'd say, "Oh, the 49ers are playing." But when you see Reggie in a green uniform now, you have to remind yourself that he's with the Packers. When you see a photo of Joe Montana in a red uniform, you have to check to see if it was a 49ers uniform or a Chiefs uniform.

You don't know who's playing for which team. Or who's going to be back next season.

At first, I just couldn't understand it all. Even when people who knew something about it tried to explain it to me, I got the feeling they didn't understand it either. It got to the point where when I started reading a newspaper about it, the sentence just blurred into a blot. Did that happen to you too? I don't know what sets it off. Maybe boredom or disinterest or just not understanding it. You know how you blot stuff out. That happens to me when I start reading about the salary cap, free agents, restricted, unrestricted. I just draw a blot.

I knew the NFL was no longer the same NFL that I knew when I leafed through the San Francisco *Chronicle* one morning and grabbed what I thought was the sports section because it had a big 49ers headline across the top. It was the business section.

Free agency was something the players complained for years about not having, but the system worked pretty well for everyone. Finally, when the players got free agency, that was the good news, but the bad news was that there was a salary cap on every club's payroll. It was like giving someone a fast car but putting a governor on it.

I used to say that you had to be a fan of the uniform, but they even messed that up in 1994 with all those "throwback" jerseys.

The idea was to commemorate the NFL's seventy-fifth season by having players wear their team's jerseys from earlier eras. Wear your home "throwback" jersey once and your road "throwback" jersey once. Nice idea. But when some teams won, like the 49ers, they kept wearing the throwback jerseys out of superstition. After a while you didn't know what the 49ers were wearing. Were they wearing throwback jerseys? Were they wearing new uniforms?

Then the Cowboys added to the confusion. Jerry Jones came up with a new jersey for special occasions. Now the Cowboys not only had blue home jerseys and white road jerseys but also throwback jerseys, even special-occasion jerseys for Super Bowl games or playoff games or Thanksgiving Day games or maybe certain Monday night games. But they were really just more Cowboy uniforms to sell to the fans.

You also never know who is going to be in those uniforms from year to year. You almost have to wait until the beginning of each season to know all the players on your team because each club has to make its payroll fit the salary cap. They even have a word for the guy in charge of the cap for each club. Capologist. He's the guy that always knows if your club's payroll has jumped over the cap or how much it's under the cap.

During the cap's first season in 1994, most of the clubs really didn't know what was going on because no one in the front office had ever dealt with it before. There was no good ol' Tommy, he's been doing cap in this league for twenty-five years. No one had been doing it. Even in the cap's third year now, some of it is still trial and error. And for a coach, it's a real trial.

Back when I coached, I never really looked at pro football as a business. I always heard people arguing, "I say it's a business, you say it's a game," or "You say it's a business, I say it's a game." In those years the only time I thought of pro football as a business was when a guy signed his contract. Once that was done, he was a player. Then it was a game again. But because I never dealt with signing players, to me it was always a game. And with the players then, it was always a game.

But with free agency now, you hear more and more players saying, "I know it's a business." And it is. But for the best players, I think it's still a game. That's one reason they're the best players.

Once their contract is signed, once their business is done, I think the best players forget about the money. During the 1994 NFC championship game, I mentioned that Rickey Jackson, the longtime Saints linebacker the 49ers had signed as a free agent, had several big bonus clauses in his contract. With the 49ers getting to the Super Bowl, he was sure of about $500,000. If they won it, he got another $300,000. Back at the hotel that night, I was in the lobby when Rickey walked in with his two sons.

"We saw your bus outside," Rickey said. "Can my boys see what your bus looks like inside?"

While his sons were in the bus, I congratulated Rickey on his bonus money, but he stared at me like he didn't know what I was talking about. I really don't think he had thought about the money until I brought it up. Even then, he didn't talk about it. He kept talking about going to the Super Bowl for the first time after all those frustrating seasons in New Orleans. He was thinking about his next game. He wasn't thinking about the business of his bonus.

There aren't enough players like that now. And the salary cap won't always let you keep those that are.

Another thing I don't like is those "player-only meetings." Anytime a team loses two in a row, they always have one of those player-only meetings that I think are the dumbest thing in sports. Just block and tackle, throw and catch. That's how you win. You don't win with meetings.

There's one more reason I couldn't coach now. Just about all the coaches wear a telephone headset; but I never did, and I never could. I would feel too restricted on the sideline with a headset on.

I know what you're thinking. I wear a headset as a broadcaster but in a television booth I'm already restricted. I can't go anywhere. On the sideline I would want to wander to where I could see what every player was doing on every play. I'd step on the cable to my headset. I'd trip on it. Back when I was coaching, I sometimes grabbed one of my assistant coach's headsets and talked into it, but I never put it on.

Then or now, I wouldn't wear a headset for three reasons: One, I wouldn't want to feel restricted. Two, I would talk too much and interrupt anyone else who was talking. Three, within the first ten minutes of the game, that headset would be broken.

HOW TO
WATCH FOOTBALL

Four or five years after I'd stopped coaching, I went to the Raiders' training camp one day and stood on the sideline when they were scrimmaging the Cowboys. After only two or three minutes, I turned to the people around me.

"Holy moly," I said. "I forgot what it was like down here."

I meant the sounds and the sights and the smells. With all that equipment the players have on, the blocking and tackling sound like two trucks colliding. Down there you hear the grunts of the players and the yells of the coaches. And you feel the weather. It was steamy hot that day, and on the sideline I could smell it.

If there's anything that I've missed since I've been in the booth, it's being on the sideline. If I had only one more game to go to in my lifetime, I'd want to watch it from the sideline and hear those sounds.

Getting those sounds is television's next responsibility. We have the pictures of what football looks like, but we don't yet have what football sounds like. When we get more microphones in more locations, we're going to get more and better sounds that we can feed into the pictures. When you have the sounds to go with the pictures, you'll be hearing it and feeling it like you never have before.

I know, you're probably worried about the choice words you might hear. But the only time we want our microphones in there is from just before the snap, when the quarterback is calling signals, until the whistle blows after the tackle. That's when you hear all the playing and the hitting. After that, we'll pull the microphones out. We don't need the choice words. We don't want them.

I'd also like to put a point on the television screen to show where the offensive team has to get for a first down. If you're sitting in the stadium, you can see the first-down markers because they're on both sides of the field. But if there's a tight shot on television, you can't always see them. I don't know technically how that point on the screen would work, but I'm sure it can be done.

Hey, technically, I don't even know how our pictures get on the air. But everywhere I go, people ask me, "When you're watching a game, what do you watch?"

My answer is always, "I don't watch the ball, and I don't watch the quarterback, at least not right away." At the snap, I watch what the center and the other offensive linemen do. If they're firing out, I know it's a running play and I'm watching to see where the hole is for the running back. If the offensive linemen are pass blocking, I watch what patterns the pass receivers are running and try to read what coverage the defensive backs are in, man-to-man or zone. And then I watch the quarterback throw.

I do all that in two or three seconds, which sounds like a short time, but it's really not.

If it's a pass, two or three seconds is plenty of time to scan what's happening because the quarterback's pass will be the last thing to happen in that progression—the snap, the blocking, the pass patterns, the read, the throw.

Try it. Don't expect to see everything right away, but the more you do it, the more you'll see.

Not everybody will want to watch a game that way. If your brother or a friend is playing, you might prefer to watch him on every play. And a mother will always watch her son on every play. Or you might prefer to watch your favorite player, the way some people just watched Joe Montana even after he handed off.

However you watch it, try to imagine what it's like being out there on the field or on the sideline.

That's where the action is. As a coach, I was down on the sideline for almost twenty years. Down there you can see when someone's getting tired. You can see when someone's fresh. You can see when someone's determined. You can see when someone's upset. You can see when someone's losing confidence.

When you can see and feel all these things, you know what your team can do or can't do. If you're near the goal line, you just know you can pump this running play into the end zone. Or if your field-goal kicker gives you that funny look, you just know he's going to miss from 51 yards. You just know.

Up in the booth, you don't see or feel those things. And you don't see or feel other things, like the wind and the weather.

On television, there's nothing more beautiful than Giants Stadium on a sunny day late in the season. The picture on your set and on my monitor in the booth is as clear as the blue sky. But you don't feel the elements and neither do I. That's why I always ask somebody in our television truck to remind me to check the flags to see how hard the wind is blowing or to tell me what the temperature is so that I can relate to what the players are coping with down on the field.

On the sideline you know all those things. You're standing there and you hear the *whoooosh* of the wind. It's blowing in your face or it's blowing at your back. You know when you're going with the wind or against the wind. When it's hot, you're sweating along with the players. When it's cold, you know the players are cold because you're freezing too. You know that there's ice along your sideline from the 20 all the way to the end zone.

But as much as I enjoy being on the sideline, the first thing I had to learn as an analyst in 1979 was how to watch a game from the booth.

After I signed on with CBS, they invited me to a seminar where I thought somebody would sit me down and tell me how to be an analyst. But all they talked about was expense reports. When they assigned me to a 49ers–Saints game, I said, "Let me a do a practice game first." Nobody had ever done that before. Now every new broadcaster does it. They call them rehearsals and they tape them. My rehearsal was a Rams–49ers game. Vince Scully and George Allen were the real announcers. I would be in another booth with Bob Costas, who was then a young CBS announcer.

The day of the game, I went out on the field at the L.A. Coliseum because I had always been on the field. I had never even watched a game from up in the coach's booth. I had always watched a game at field level, so that's where I went.

Before I left the field, I did what television calls a stand-up. I stood there with a microphone and talked about the game, then I went upstairs to the booth. But when the game started, everything was so far away, I didn't know what I was watching. This wasn't the same game I'd been watching all those years on the sideline. The big difference was that I couldn't talk to any players to find out what was going on, what they were seeing.

I had always coached by asking my players questions and reacting to what they told me, to how they felt, to how they looked. To me, that was football. Everyone together.

That's the way I coached. But in the booth that day, I suddenly felt detached.

Until then I had always been on the field as a player, then as an assistant coach at a junior college, a head coach at a junior college, an assistant coach at San Diego State, an assistant coach with the Raiders, and as a head coach with the Raiders. But now that I was detached up in the booth, I knew I had to find some way to reattach myself. That way was the big television monitor next to me.

During a play I learned to watch all twenty-two players on the field, just as I had when I was coaching, then to look at the monitor to see what's on the screen. Sometimes when a wide receiver catches a pass near the far sideline, all I see is a bunch of guys, but when I look at the monitor, I'll know who he is.

Another thing I had to learn was how to watch a game standing close to the monitor. All your life you're taught to stand away from a television screen, that you'll go blind from the rays or whatever. But after my rehearsal game, CBS sent me a tape. I didn't have a VCR then. I didn't even know what a VCR was. I had to find someplace to go watch it so I went to Channel 2 in Oakland and they set it up for me. Watching the tape, I couldn't believe how terrible I was. I had no idea what I was doing.

But as bad as I was, after I did my first real game the next week, the 49ers–Saints game at Candlestick Park, I knew this was what I wanted to do.

Not the television part, because I'm still not big on the television part, but I liked being around football and being a guy that could go to the games with a job to do. The job part was important. During the 1979 preseason I went to a Raiders game, but I didn't know where to go or what to do. I couldn't even sit and watch. I ended up walking around and leaving. I never went to another game until I started doing television, and what made me feel good about doing television was that now I had a reason to go to a game. I had a job there.

I'm not like that at other sports events. I've got season tickets to the Oakland A's and the Golden State Warriors and I can sit there and enjoy the games. I go to fights. One of my favorite things is to go to big fights in Las Vegas. But with football, I guess because it's always been my life and my job, I couldn't go to a game without having a job there. And with television, I had a job there.

To do that job right, I had to learn to talk about what you the viewer are seeing, not what I might have seen. Just as you the viewer have no choice as to what you're watching, I have no choice about what I should be talking about. You're going to watch what our director, Sandy Grossman, is showing you, and I'm going to talk about what he's showing you. Most of the time that's a play in the game. But sometimes it might be the six-legged turkey in my bus on Thanksgiving Day or a seagull perched in the rafters near the end of a 49ers game in San Francisco.

I'm always being asked, "What do you see?" and I always say, "I see the same thing you see," meaning the same picture.

Someday there will be interactive television where you'll be able to sit home and decide what you want to see—the usual view from the 50-yard line or the view from the end zone or the view from a camera isolated on the quarterback or the view from a sideline camera. But until then, you and I will be seeing the same picture. When the play starts, I try to see what all twenty-two players are doing. I can't just watch two or three players. I've got to watch the whole play, because if I just watch two or three players, they may not be in the replay. In watching the whole play, I might see the left tackle miss his block, but if the replay is showing the wide receiver running his pass pattern, I can't talk about the left tackle missing his block.

During the replay, I've got to talk about what the wide receiver is doing.

That's the good thing about the Telestrator. If I said, "The 49ers are using three wide receivers here with Jerry Rice in the slot," some viewers wouldn't know that Jerry Rice's number is eighty or where the slot is, but if I circle Jerry Rice with the Telestrator, the gray-haired guy who played football in high school and the kid who's watching a game for the first time, they're both on the same page with me.

Matchups are trickier. Some people think there's a matchup when there isn't a matchup. Reggie White, the Packers' left defensive end, might be matched up against Erik Williams, the Cowboys' right offensive tackle, on most plays, but sometimes Reggie will line up over the center or over one of the guards. If he gets a sack lined up there, you can't blame Erik Williams. With a pass rusher who moves around like Reggie does, I always try to check where he's lined up on every play so I know what the matchup is.

But if you're like I was even as a rookie offensive tackle with the Eagles in 1959, you have to learn how to watch football.

When I played at Jefferson Union High School or at San Mateo (California) Junior College, the University of Oregon, Grays Harbor College (in Aberdeen, Washington), and Cal Poly in San Luis Obispo, I never knew what football was all about. I never really understood it. All I knew was what I did as an offensive lineman, and what guys at my position did. I think most players are that way. I didn't know what linebackers or defensive backs did. I just knew who I blocked and how to try to block him. I wasn't a kid that studied football. I just wanted to go to a 49ers game, then come home and try to copy what the pros did and how they did it.

I grew up in Daly City, near the San Francisco city line, not too far from Kezar Stadium in Golden Gate Park. I was maybe eleven years old when I first started going to 49ers games with my pal John Robinson, now Southern Cal's coach and the former Los Angeles Rams coach.

In those years, there were no freeways, no big parking lots. To get to Kezar, we hopped a bus or a streetcar or we hitchhiked. I don't know anyone who hitchhikes now, but those were different days. We'd stick our thumbs out, and a guy would pick us up, take us as far as he was going and drop us. It might take two or three rides to get close, then we'd walk to the stadium, hang around outside, and watch all the players come in. The games always started at one, but we were there by ten, and they didn't start taking tickets until twelve, so there weren't many security guards around. When we thought nobody was looking, we'd run through the gate. We were in the stadium. Then we'd take a seat. If someone came with a ticket for that seat, we'd move to another seat. We just kept moving until nobody came. After the game we would run out on the field to be with the players. Just stand there and hear them talking to each other.

In those years, the 49ers had a player named Charley Powell, who was right out of high school. Some of the pros hadn't gone to college, but they had played for Army, Navy, or Marine teams at military bases. Charley joined the 49ers right out of high school in San Diego.

That was a hard one for me to relate to. I always thought of pros as guys who had played in college or in the service and were seven or eight years older than I was, but here was this big guy, six feet two and 228 pounds, right out of high school playing tight end, defensive end, and linebacker. What I remember best about him was that he taped his hands like a boxer. In fact, he later was a pretty good heavyweight. He taped his hands up past his wrists. Seeing him do it, I wanted to tape my hands.

Being a lineman, I wanted to be an offensive and defensive tackle like Bob Toneff of the 49ers. He could run.

He could really move. I always looked for him on the field after the game.

One time I was walking near John Henry Johnson, the 49ers' fullback, when a woman came up to him, squealed, "John Henry, John Henry," and went to kiss him. He turned around, all sweaty and dirty, but he had no teeth. His false teeth were in his locker. She screeched, "*Arrrgggghhh*," and ran away. But he looked like John Henry to me, like the toughest guy I'd ever seen.

Another time I was walking off the field near Harland Svare, a Rams linebacker. When somebody asked him for his autograph, he said, "I'm sorry, I can't. I'm just too tired and too beat up." I never asked for an autograph. I just wanted to be with the players, to be near them, to walk like them. I thought I was always going to play. I never thought about coaching or doing television or getting hurt. I was the same way in college. I thought I'd play forever. When the Eagles signed me as a tackle in 1959, I thought I was indestructible.

But in practice one day, a pile of guys fell across my left knee from behind. Just tore it all up. When you had surgery for torn knee ligaments and torn cartilage in those days, you were done for the season.

The doctor told me, "Maybe you can play next year." I didn't like that "maybe," but the Eagles kept me around all season to rehab my knee. In the morning I'd get to Franklin Field early so I'd be out of the whirlpool before the real players arrived for practice. Norm Van Brocklin, the Dutchman, the quarterback who would lead the Eagles to the 1960 NFL championship, was the only other player there that early. He'd go into a little room, sit next to a rickety old movie projector, and watch game films.

"Hey, Red," he called to me one day, "c'mon in and sit down."

I pulled up a stool and sat in the back. Whenever I watched films before that, I'd been like most players. I just watched myself or the guy on the other team I had to block. So when the Dutchman invited me to watch films with him, I really didn't know what I was watching. But since I was the only one in there with him, he started talking to me.

"You see that," he would say. "You see that."

I hadn't seen anything. He had seen everything.

"I think we can get that post," he would say.

After a few days, he turned to where I was sitting in the back and said, "C'mon up here and watch this with me." He never wanted any feedback. I never said, "Why didn't you do this?" But from then on, he kept talking even more, really explaining what he was looking for. He was always trying to do what his best players could do. He was always looking to see how he could throw deep to Tommy McDonald, how he could throw short to Bobby Walston, how he could throw over the middle to Pete Retzlaff, how he could throw a swing pass to Clarence Peaks.

"To understand what you want to do offensively," he told me, "you had to understand the defenses."

He taught me how to recognize what the defensive backs and linebackers were doing. I learned zone and man-to-man, and combination coverages. To attack those defenses, I learned how to use different pass patterns: ins, outs, comebacks, hooks, posts, ups. Sitting there watching the film, he would read the coverage and tell me what he could do against it.

"The way they play this zone," he would say, "Retzlaff can get behind the linebacker."

As an offensive lineman all my life, I already knew the techniques for those positions. How to run block, how to pass block, how to pull and trap. Now I was learning offense and defense. I knew I was ten years behind the Dutchman, who would later coach the Vikings and the Falcons, but ten years behind him was ten years ahead of anyone else my age. Sitting in that little room, I had learned how to attack and defend. That really got me thinking about being a coach, and when I went back to Cal Poly in San Luis Obispo, I knew I had to get my teacher's credentials.

In 1960 I was student teaching at the junior high school when San Luis Obispo High School needed a football coach. The coach from the year before had left and the new coach, Jack Frost, hadn't arrived yet. The athletic director, Phil Prijatel, knew I had played at Cal Poly and had been with the Eagles, so he asked me to handle spring football. I was only twenty-two, but after all I had learned from Norm Van Brocklin, I knew I could coach the whole team all by myself and I did.

I had fifty kids out there, but I coached everyone—the quarterback, the running backs, the pass receivers, the offensive line, the defensive line, the linebackers, the defensive backs, the kickers, the punters, everybody. Jack Frost sent me his playbook, and I put in his offense and defense. Looking back, I don't know how I did it, but I did it. Looking back, now that I know what I had to do, I never would have done it; but I knew I could coach all these kids all by myself. I really thought I knew everything. I thought I was the smartest young football guy there was, but I had more confidence than I had knowledge or talent.

As an assistant coach and then the head coach at Alan Hancock Junior College in Santa Maria, California, I thought I really knew football. But in the summer of 1963 I found out how little I knew.

When I heard that Vince Lombardi would be speaking at a coaching seminar at the University of Nevada in Reno, I couldn't enroll fast enough. He was going to talk about the Lombardi Sweep, which he had made famous in Green Bay: Paul Hornung taking a hand-off from Bart Starr and running to his right or left behind the blocking of fullback Jim Taylor and the two guards who had pulled out of the line, Jerry Kramer and Fuzzy Thurston.

But as much as I just wanted to see and hear Vince Lombardi up close, hey, I was a football coach too. I thought I knew everything about football. Until he started talking.

He stood up there with a piece of chalk in his hand and drew the play on the blackboard. He showed film. One by one, he pretended he was each of his eleven players and explained what each of them did on the play. Not only against one defense, but against several defenses.

He spent eight hours talking about one play. Eight hours. That's when I realized I might have a lot to learn about coaching football.

I kept learning. I went back to Hancock for that 1963 season. In 1964 I moved to San Diego State as the defensive coordinator under Don Coryell (who later coached the St. Louis Cardinals and the San Diego Chargers). I joined the Raiders in 1967 as their linebacker coach, then from 1969 through 1978 I was the Raiders' head coach. And I learned something every day.

One of the things I learned from Jim Otto, the Raiders' Hall of Fame center, was how a great pro watches game films. In college and in the pros, the average player's reaction to seeing himself miss a block would be to put his head down or turn away. He doesn't want to see himself missing that block again and again as the coach with the clicker runs the play back and forth ten or twenty times.

But when I joined the Raiders, I noticed that when Jim Otto missed a block, instead of putting his head down or turning away, he would say, "Run that again." He'd watch that play five or six times. He wanted to see his mistakes. He expected to make a good block. He wanted to see what happened when he missed a block. That's a great pro.

As the Raiders' head coach, I had a rule that the players had to watch things they didn't want to see and listen to things they didn't want to hear with the same enthusiasm that they watched the things they liked to see and listened to the things they liked to hear. It's like with schoolkids in a classroom. You're trying to teach them, not embarrass them. You can't let players think you're trying to embarrass them or make fun of them. You've got to do it in the same kind of voice as when you're praising them for a good play. As a coach, you've got to be able to criticize a player and still have his respect. And the player has to be able to accept that criticism and learn from it so he doesn't make the same mistake again.

It was the same with watching film as a coach. You had to see why a play didn't work so that the next time it would work. Maybe it was the wrong play against the defense the other team was in. Maybe it was the right play but a defensive guy made a great play. So you're always looking to see what you did wrong and what you did right. But, whether you're a coach or a player or a fan, it all comes back to just watching football the way you want to watch it.

CHANGING
CHANNELS TO FOX

When the phone rang on my bus that Friday afternoon going to Detroit for a 49ers–Lions game late in the 1993 season, I had no idea what Sandy Montag, my agent at the International Management Group, was about to tell me.

"Fox got the NFC package," he said. "CBS is out."

I couldn't believe it. During the week Janis Delson, then the director of broadcasting at CBS Sports, had told me about the rumor that Fox might get the NFC package for the 1994–1997 seasons, but I shot it down.

"I know how the NFL works," I told her. "If a new network wants in, they'll arrange a new package for it."

That's how it always had been done. Back when ABC wanted in for the 1970 season, the NFL offered them the Monday night package. When ESPN wanted in, they got the Sunday night package, and when TNT wanted in, they shared the Sunday night package with ESPN.

"Fox will get some kind of new package," I told Janis, "but they won't get the NFC away from CBS."

Long before I started at CBS, it had televised the NFL

games that evolved in 1970 into the National Conference package while NBC had the American Conference package. I couldn't imagine the National Conference games with all the old teams like the Cowboys, 49ers, Redskins, Giants, and Bears being anywhere but on the CBS network.

But when Fox offered $1.58 billion over four years and CBS offered $1.04 billion, CBS was out. That meant I was out too.

According to my contract, if CBS didn't have pro football, I would be released. But I really wasn't thinking much about what I would be doing the next season.

"I'll start thinking about it after the Super Bowl," I told people.

"You don't have the Super Bowl this year, John," somebody reminded me.

"You're right, the NFC championship is our last game," I said, "but I just want to enjoy the rest of the games I'm doing for CBS."

"But where do you think you'll be next season?"

"I'll see what happens after all this settles."

I meant it. I didn't want to disrupt my concentration on the games I still had to do. While we were working the 49ers–Lions game that Sunday, CBS made a late bid to get the AFC package away from NBC, but it was too late. In the preliminary negotiations CBS had told the NFL that it wasn't interested in the AFC package. Even though CBS now was bidding more than NBC had, the NFL decided that they owed the AFC package to NBC.

CBS was out of pro football unless it could organize a new league. For a few days I thought that might happen. I still think it should have happened. That's how the old American Football League got started in 1960. The situation was right. There was a network available. Some good players were free agents. Some good cities and good owners were there. But when a new league didn't happen, I knew I needed a job.

I knew the other networks were possibilities for me. Maybe Fox, maybe NBC, maybe ABC in their Monday night booth. But I didn't think anything was about to happen right away. I did my last regular-season game, the Cowboys–Giants game on January 2 at Giant Stadium, then I stayed in my New York apartment with my son Mike the next week while waiting to do the Giants–Vikings wild-card playoff the following Sunday.

One night that week I had three messages on my answering machine. One from Rupert Murdoch, one from Steve Wynn, one from Bob Halloran.

Murdoch, the owner of the Fox television network, was at a convention in Las Vegas, staying at the Mirage, which Steve Wynn owns and where Bob Halloran was his vice president. When I called Bob back, he told me that Murdoch wanted to meet me. When I talked to Murdoch, he told me he would be in New York that weekend.

"Why don't you stop by my apartment and say hello," he said. "I'd like to meet you."

I thought, *Hey, I'd like to meet you.* Not to talk about a job. Just to meet the guy I'd heard and read so much about. Just to meet the guy who decided to pay more than a billion and a half dollars to put pro football games on television. No matter who it is, I'd rather hear other people tell me about what they do than me tell them what I do. I'd rather hear a farmer talk about raising crops or cattle or hear a fisherman talk about catching fish. I've learned that with farmers or fishermen, something's always wrong. With farmers either it rained too much or it didn't rain enough. With fishermen, either they're catching too many fish and the price is down or they're not catching any fish and not making any money. So when Rupert Murdoch wanted to meet me, I wanted to meet him.

"I'm free Sunday night," I told him. "I can be there about eight."

He gave me the address of his Central Park South

apartment. After the Giants–Vikings playoff game, Mike and I had dinner in a Mexican restaurant near my Manhattan apartment, then I started to walk over to see Rupert Murdoch.

"Are you going like that?" Mike said.

I was wearing a baseball cap, a leather jacket over a white shirt, khakis, and sneakers. I had taken my tie off as soon as we were off camera.

"I did the game in these sneakers," I said. "That's what I wear."

Hey, that's me. I wasn't going to change my clothes to impress Rupert Murdoch. At the time I thought I'd be going to either NBC or ABC, but I knew just being able to talk to him for a couple of hours would be interesting. His Australia-based News Corporation is involved in television in the United States, Europe, and Asia. It also operates the Twentieth Century Fox movie studios, the *New York Post* and other newspapers, as well as the HarperCollins book publishing company. According to *Forbes* magazine, he's worth $4 billion. And he lives like it. The elevator in his building didn't just go up to a floor with other apartments. It went up to his apartment, the only one on that floor. His living room looked out over Central Park and as soon as I walked in, a waiter asked me what I wanted to drink and offered me some hors d'oeuvres. I just sat in a chair with a Diet Coke.

When Rupert Murdoch walked in, he was wearing a dark business suit. As we talked, I think I wanted to know more about him than he wanted to know about me. One of the first things I said was, "What did you do today?"

He went over his whole day. He had talked to his London newspaper about an editorial. He had talked to his people at the *New York Post.* He had talked to other people about television satellites and about television going interactive. He's really an electronics guy. He's thinking about what the future will be like in television, in newspapers, in everything he has going.

But the one thing I really wanted to know was how he decided to offer the NFL that $1.58 billion.

"There is a point where the NFL just can't turn us down," he said. "If we made an offer that was just a little above what CBS was offering, the NFL's loyalty to CBS wouldn't have been affected. Our offer was divisible by the twenty-eight clubs. If our offer was only $28 million more, that's only $1 million more a club. That's not worth the NFL's loyalty to a network it had been in business with all these years. We had to come up with a number that made the owners say, 'We just can't turn this amount of money down.'"

That money was $395 million a year for four years. In the previous contract, CBS had been paying $265 million a year.

Murdoch knew CBS was "grudgingly prepared," as he has said, to go over $300 million a year, but he didn't know how much over. So he decided to go for what he has described as "the knockout bid" of nearly $400 million. What impressed me was that his whole thinking process is different from mine, and different from that of most people. He goes out and gets something, then figures out how to make it work. Most people figure out how to make something work, then go out and get it.

Does the suit fit? Yes, then I'll buy it. But he buys the suit, then makes it fit.

Fox didn't have any sports and he wanted to get into sports. Most networks would do some golf first, some figure skating, some boxing, maybe some hockey. But he went, *boom*, NFL football. He took on CBS for the NFC games, and he got it. But the whole time I was there, he never brought up anything about me working at Fox, and I never brought it up. He hadn't made me an offer, and I knew he wouldn't. With all the people involved in negotiations these days, that's not the way it's done. When I left, we shook hands and I said, "Maybe we'll see each other down the road." I didn't mean anything by it. Like I say, at the time I thought I would be going to NBC or ABC, and the only reason I went to see him was that I just wanted to meet him.

I went back to my apartment where Mike was waiting, then we got on the bus to go home for the 49ers–Giants playoff on Saturday at Candlestick Park.

By the time we got home, Barry Frank and Sandy Montag were calling to tell me that NBC and ABC each had come up with more money than I was making at CBS, and then Fox got into it. But it really wasn't about money. It was about wanting to do the same NFC games with the same people in the same cities with the same teams and the same players. I know that's hard to believe with the amount of money I was being offered, but I had enjoyed being in the booth with Pat Summerall for so long and I had enjoyed having Bob Stenner as our producer and Sandy Grossman as our director for so long, I just wanted the whole deal to stay that way.

The more Fox talked, the more they were ready to hire Pat and Bob and Sandy along with Ed Goren as our executive producer and Janis Delson as vice president for football programming and talent. Fox knew they needed the best people and these were the best people. That was part of the Fox plan, and I liked that part. I knew I'd be comfortable because I'd always enjoyed working with these people.

Not long after I signed, I went to a press thing in Los Angeles to introduce Fox Sports but on the way into it, I said, "There shouldn't be an s on the end. It should just be Fox Sport." They only had one sport, pro football. Then we had a meeting in my Pleasanton, California, office to talk about how to put this together. David Hill, the president of Fox Sports, came up with George Krieger, the executive vice president, along with Ed Goren and Janis Delson. To me, the most important thing was to work on getting the best possible schedule of games.

The way the NFL television package works, Fox gets all the games between NFC teams along with the games when an NFC team is visiting an AFC team while NBC gets all the games between AFC teams along with the games when an AFC team is visiting an NFC team. So we knew what games we were going to get minus the Monday night games that ABC got and the Sunday night games that ESPN and TNT got.

To me, the best possible games have always been a big thing. That's what Rupert Murdoch paid a billion and a half dollars for—the games. That's our product. So we rated the games and then we talked about what we wanted to do in the preseason. By the time we had a symposium in Los Angeles, we were talking about how we wanted to cover the games, but we didn't have all our announcers for the other games. I kept wondering if we were going to pull it off. But the more meetings we had with David Hill, the better I felt.

David is an Australian who had worked for Rupert Murdoch in London as the head of Sky Sports and earlier he had been with Eurosport, doing soccer, auto racing, horse racing, golf, tennis, and rugby on television. He not only understands sports, but he's a brilliant idea guy.

What impressed me about David, he's very loose, he's very bright, and he's open to anything. If you bring up an idea, and I've always been one that had a lot of ideas, a lot of people, their first thought is, you can't do it. David's approach is how you can do it. Which I really like because most people are the opposite of that. Especially in the television business. David has a fresh new outlook on how to do pro football. He'd never been around it or with a network that did it, so when something came up about making the sound better, the coverage better, the camera work better, he wouldn't say, "Well, when I did NFL games, we didn't do that," because he had never done NFL games. He didn't have an old way of doing them.

At a Fox symposium in Los Angeles a few months later, we started off talking about graphics and I mentioned, "We get so carried away with graphics and what's going on in other games that we don't give our own score and time often enough. How often when you're sitting home watching a game, the phone rings and you'll tell the person on the other end that you're watching a game and you hear, 'What's the score?' and you say, 'I don't know.' That's the way people at home are. We're showing the scores of other games and how many yards someone has, but we're not giving the score of our game often enough. I think the one thing we ought to do, we ought to put the score and the time on the screen more often. I think it ought to be banged in there every sixty seconds, maybe every thirty seconds."

Across the room, David Hill looked over and said, "Why don't we just put it in there and leave it in there all the time." Everybody just looked at each other. Nobody had thought of doing it that way before, so Fox originated that little box up in the corner of the screen with the score and the time left in the quarter. It's worked out great. In a Fox game you always know what the score is and how much time is left. All because David Hill was willing to try it.

In addition to Pat Summerall, Fox quickly hired Terry Bradshaw, Jimmy Johnson, and Howie Long for the pregame show along with Dick Stockton and Matt Millen as game announcers.

The day Jimmy Johnson and Jerry Jones announced their split, Ed Goren and David Hill were in New York watching ESPN's coverage of the Cowboys' news conference. Without even mentioning Jimmy's name, Ed turned to David and said, "I'll see you in a few days."

"When you get a chance, check in," David said.

On the plane to Dallas later that afternoon, Ed phoned Jimmy, whom he had known from when Jimmy occasionally appeared on CBS's college football show.

"Guess who's coming to dinner," Ed said.

"Guess who's not coming to dinner," Jimmy said. "I've been a coach for thirty years, and now I'm not a coach. I'm not talking to anybody tonight."

"How about breakfast?" Ed asked.

That morning the negotiations began. Several weeks later Jimmy Johnson agreed to turn down a generous ESPN offer. All the anticipation of Fox putting together a staff of announcers, production people, and technicians to staff as many as six or seven games on a Sunday was exciting. I think we all need excitement in our lives. The excitement was that Fox had never done it before, but it wasn't as wild and crazy as if you had never done it with these people because most of the announcers, production crews, and technicians had worked for CBS on pro football. It was the best of both worlds. It was something new, and yet most of us had done it before.

But for Fox, it was all new. Fox had never really had a network. It had entertainment from eight to ten at night, that was it; and for our first preseason game on August 12, there was just Pat and me, Bob and Sandy, along with some of our old CBS production crew and technicians in Candlestick Park for the 49ers and the Broncos.

I remember standing in the booth, getting ready to do the game, looking at my monitor and hearing the countdown in my headset, "ten . . . nine . . . eight . . . seven," and thinking, *I hope something comes up on the screen;* "six . . . five . . . four," and thinking, *There was no pregame show, we were the first thing on, this is going to be a historic moment, the NFL on Fox;* "three . . . two . . . one . . ." and then I saw the Fox logo with the music.

I pushed my "cough" key and told Bob and Sandy, "We made air."

Our team of announcers, production people, and technicians did two more preseason games in New Orleans and Chicago, but when the season started, Fox had a real network. Our game, the Cowboys in Pittsburgh, was one of six Fox televised that Sunday afternoon. The next day I called David Hill.

"How did it work out?" I asked.

"It all went off great," he said.

We were both excited. Hey, we did it. We made it work. In life, I'm always amazed by how things work. When I'm in San Francisco I'm always amazed how they get that many people in and out over the Golden Gate Bridge and the Bay Bridge. When I'm in New York City, I'm always amazed how all those people get there in the morning and get out at night and how, over the years, no one ever messed up Central Park right there in the middle of Manhattan, that some administration didn't sell off a piece of it so somebody could build condos or an office building. And with Fox, I was amazed that the whole thing started from scratch in February and that in September we had a network of NFL games. Everybody from David Hill and Ed Goren on down, they all did the job. And the excitement of the unknown made it a fun thing.

The second year, we grew and at the end of the 1996 season Fox Sports will be doing its first Super Bowl. And now that it's doing baseball, hockey, and boxing, it's really Fox Sports.

For me, one of the best parts about Fox is being able to keep working with Pat Summerall, the easiest guy in the world to get along with. No matter what comes up, he'll say, "No problem." Somebody will tell him, "We just got a call from the pregame show, they want you to . . ." Pat will say, "No problem." Or somebody will tell him, "We have to leave at six in the morning." Pat will say, "No problem, I'll be there." No matter what it is, he never gets upset about anything. He's not only easy to be around, he's fun to be around. Every time you see him, he always has a joke or a story that makes you laugh.

Some of our viewers don't even know that he was a place kicker and a tight end with the Giants and before that with the Chicago Cardinals. He kicked a famous 50-yard field goal in the snow at Yankee Stadium that put the Giants into an Eastern Conference playoff before their sudden-death overtime loss to the Colts in the 1958 NFL championship game also at Yankee Stadium.

Pat has respect for everything and everybody—the players, the coaches, the television people. And when people tell me that we blend so well together, I always say, "He's the reason." He gives me freedom to say whatever I want, because when I'm done, he'll sum it up and make sense out of it and get it back to where we have to go with the next play. He'll do it so smoothly and effortlessly, some people don't even realize it.

But I do.

A PLAN FOR BETTER OFFICIATING

Wherever I go in pro football, I hear people complaining about the officiating being bad. Sometimes it is. But that's because the NFL needs to redo its whole structure of officiating. When new rules are put in, tell the guys in the striped shirts how to call those rules. Hire full-time officials. Install a quicker and better form of instant replay. Stay on top of the officiating problem during the off-season.

The way it is now, too many situations in pro football are just about impossible to officiate. That's why it's hard for me to be critical of the officials during a game.

When I see a bad call during a game, I react to it. But when I think about it later, I know it's unfair to be critical of someone who doesn't have a chance to succeed.

When the NFL Competition Committee of coaches, general managers, and owners meets in March, they go over everything that went wrong the season before and propose rule changes, usually to help the offense score more points. Then the owners vote on the changes and dump the new rules on the officials and say, "Here's the game, you officiate it."

But no one ever considers how you're supposed to call the rules. Especially the ones you really can't call. Like the roughing-the-passer rule.

The way the rule reads is: "No defensive player may run into a passer of a legal forward pass after the ball has left his hand. The referee must determine whether the opponent had a reasonable chance to stop his momentum during an attempt to block the pass or tackle the passer while he still had the ball." But the problem is, the referee has to make a subjective judgment on the pass rusher's "reasonable chance" to stop his momentum. One referee's subjective judgment will be different from another referee's subjective judgment. One player gets penalized, then he gets fined by the NFL office. Another player doesn't get penalized, but he might get fined. I don't think the players know what they can do or can't do.

My solution doesn't involve subjective judgment. My solution is objective—a pass rusher wouldn't be allowed to "run into or rough" the passer, just as a punt rusher isn't allowed to run into or rough the punter.

Hey, once the punter punts the ball, if you touch him, it's a penalty. Punt rushers have learned to live with that rule. With the quarterback, it would be the same thing. Once he releases the ball, if you touch him, it's a penalty. Now if he starts to run or he's outside the pocket, he's on his own, just like a punter or a kicker is if he starts to run. But if the quarterback stays in the pocket, as soon as he throws the ball, the referee blows a horn, a *hoonnnk* that sounds different from a whistle. After that horn sounds, if anybody runs into or roughs the passer, it's a penalty.

Some people will say that I want to put skirts on the quarterbacks, but I say that the NFL is only as good as its good quarterbacks, and the way good quarterbacks are getting banged around, they're an endangered species.

Another rule the officials don't call consistently is pass interference. After the pass receiver goes 5 yards, the defensive player covering him can't touch him no matter what. If the pass is in the air and the defender touches him, just touches him, the rule says that's defensive pass interference. If the pass receiver touches the defender after 5 yards, that's offensive pass interference.

Every once in a while a cornerback or a safety, just by touching a pass receiver downfield, will create what amounts to a 50-yard penalty. When that happens, I'll yell, "Well, he did touch him, but it shouldn't be a 50-yard penalty." But the rule isn't, no harm, no foul. The rule is, you can't do it. So there's really no way to call it.

Sometimes when a pass receiver really gets belted, the official doesn't call a penalty. He'll say, "The receiver couldn't have caught the ball anyway." So officials mess with the players' minds so much, it gets to where the game can't be officiated.

Offensive holding is another one. At some point in pass protection, an offensive lineman is almost always going to hold a pass rusher. Sometimes, and I've been arguing this ever since I started coaching the Raiders in 1969, if the offensive lineman's upper arm is a few inches away from his body and the pass rusher puts his hand under there, that's considered offensive holding. But it shouldn't be. The pass rusher put his hand in there.

Yes, I think there's some sort of holding by offensive linemen on almost every pass rush, but I don't think there's illegal holding on every play.

I think at some point in every pass rush, there's going to be a hold that an official could call. But the problem is, if you let officials be subjective in their calls, there'll be inconsistency. One official is calling it, but another official is not. Pretty soon the offensive linemen don't know what the rules are.

When the NFL tells its officials, "The calls must be consistent, they must be standard," that brings objectivity but no understanding.

That's the dilemma no one really addresses. When the coaches and players gripe during the season, the NFL can't change the rules in midseason but they say they'll discuss it in the off-season. And they do. But once they put in the new rules, they forget about the officials. So does everybody else. In the off-season people in pro football talk about the college draft and the free agents. Nobody talks about how the officials are going to call the new rules.

Take the rule about 15-yard penalties for using the helmet as a weapon. If a passer is standing there and he's leveled with a helmet, they can call that. Or if a ball carrier is down and he's speared with a helmet, they can call that.

But they can't call it if it happens to a running back with the ball or a pass receiver with the ball after the catch, because the tackler is just trying to do anything he can to stop him. If the tackler gets a hand on the running back or the pass receiver, he's happy.

The rule was put in because of several concussions suffered by players during the 1994 season, mostly quarterbacks. Just a little concussion, some teams like to say. But there's no such thing as a little concussion. If you suffer a concussion, it means your brain has been bruised. Sometimes you're knocked out. Sometimes you're just confused, with or without temporary amnesia. No matter what, there's nothing little about a concussion. Nothing funny about it. If a guy hurts his knee or his shoulder, nobody laughs about it. But a guy with a concussion, ho ho, he's just had his bell rung. He doesn't even know where he is. He doesn't even know what day it is.

When the team doctor holds up two fingers in front of

the guy's face, he's saying, "How many fingers do you see?" Some people think that's funny. But if you're the guy trying to focus on those two fingers, it's not funny.

In boxing, the most anarchic sport of all, state athletic commissions have a rule that if a boxer is knocked out in a bout in their state, he's automatically suspended from fighting there for thirty days, sometimes sixty days.

In football, if a guy is knocked out in the first half, you sometimes hear his team talking about maybe he'll be back for the second half. Doctors will tell you that's all right if a guy is just confused without any loss of memory, but not if a guy is suffering from temporary amnesia or has been knocked unconscious. At a 1994 symposium on football safety, Dr. James P. Kelly, the director of the Rehabilitation Institute of Chicago's brain injury program, listed three grades of concussions with guidelines for a player's return.

> GRADE 1: *Confusion without amnesia and no loss of consciousness.* The player should be removed from the game, examined immediately and every five minutes for amnesia and postconcussion symptoms. He may return if amnesia does not appear and no symptoms develop for at least twenty minutes.
>
> GRADE 2: *Confusion with amnesia and no loss of consciousness.* The player should be removed from the game and not allowed to return. He should be examined frequently and reexamined the next day. He may return to practice only after one full week without any postconcussion symptoms.
>
> GRADE 3: *Loss of consciousness.* The player should be transported by ambulance to the nearest hospital for thorough neurologic evaluation. He should remain hospitalized if signs of pathology are detected and may return to practice only after two full weeks without any postconcussion symptoms.

Troy Aikman knows all about concussions. In his first six seasons as the Cowboys' quarterback, he had six. He suffered one in the 1993 NFC championship game against the 49ers, but that year there was only one week before the Super Bowl instead of the usual two weeks. When the Cowboys routed the Bills 30–13 at the Georgia Dome in Atlanta, he completed nineteen of twenty-seven passes for 207 yards with only one interception. He was sacked twice, but realized later that he didn't remember much about the second half.

"I was lucky I wasn't hit seriously in that game," he has said. "That could've been disastrous."

Chris Miller, Merril Hoge, and Al Toon weren't that lucky. Concussions forced them to stop playing.

Miller, the Rams' quarterback, took the 1996 season off after suffering five concussions in fourteen months.

During the 1994 season Hoge, the Bears' fullback, had two concussions within forty-one days. After the second one, which he suffered making a routine block, he was in the Bears' medical room at Soldier Field when doctors couldn't tell if he was breathing. His eyes had rolled to the back of his head and he wasn't responding to anything.

"I could have died," Hoge has said. "I think the doctors were really, really scared. They told me I dodged a bullet."

Hoge didn't want to dodge any more bullets. He suddenly stopped playing football. During the 1992 season Toon, the Jets' wide receiver, stopped playing after his tenth concussion. I'm told he still has headaches and dizziness.

But it's not just pro football. According to Dr. Kelly, surveys indicate that "10 percent of college football players and 20 percent of high school football players experience concussions in a given season." That adds up to more than 250,000 concussions a season. Not a number to laugh about.

The number of bad calls in any NFL season isn't that high, but a quicker and better form of instant replay would eliminate most of those bad calls.

The way the NFL used instant replay from 1986 through 1991 didn't really work but that doesn't mean it shouldn't be back. And maybe it will be. In a few selected 1996 preseason games the NFL experimented with a new instant-replay system. During the 1996 season the NFL planned to gather information on new technology in instant-replay without affecting the games themselves.

Depending on the results, maybe the NFL will vote to use a new instant-replay system for the 1997 season.

We have instant replay as such anyway. If there's a controversial play, it's always going to be replayed for everybody to see. It's going to be shown to everyone watching at home. It's going to be shown to all the writers watching in the press box. It's going to be shown to the coaches and the players and the spectators watching the big screens in the stadium. It's going to be shown that Sunday night on your local channel. It's going to be shown Monday night. If it involves your team and it's controversial enough, it's going to be shown all week.

It's also up there on the big screens in the stadium for the officials to look at too, if they want to peek. But they can't use it. If the NFL wants to get the call right, there should be a way for them to use it.

With the technology available now, there's no reason why the NFL can't develop an instant-replay procedure that would be quicker than before, that would shorten the delays that turned off so many fans. But the return of instant replay should be part of a whole new package of getting younger officials out there on the field and in the replay booth. During those six seasons of instant replays, the official in the booth was usually an old retired guy squinting at the screen. Little kids who play video games could have done a better job.

Players come into the NFL at twenty-one, twenty-two, or twenty-three; but officials don't get there until their late thirties or early forties. And some stay into their late fifties, even into their sixties. Nobody knows for sure how old they are because the NFL doesn't release their ages, just their years of experience as NFL officials.

What happens is, an official usually starts by working high-school games, then small colleges, then major colleges before he gets to be one of the best. But before the NFL will even consider him, he has to have officiated college games for at least ten years. There should be a way for the NFL to develop ex-players into officials instead of always relying on hiring college officials.

More than anything else, I think the NFL should have full-time officials. The excuse has always been that these guys couldn't leave their good jobs. But paying these guys big money shouldn't be an issue, not in the NFL with all its money.

The way to do it would be to make all their referees full-time guys at first, then a year or two later make all the umpires full-time guys. If a guy doesn't want to be a full-time guy, fine, but he can't be a referee or an umpire. Eventually, you make the third official a full-time guy, then the fourth guy. Make the fifth and sixth officials entry-level positions. And get more younger guys, especially umpires. The umpire is the guy who stands right there behind the defensive line and he really gets knocked around. Usually you don't even see it because the ball and the cameras are somewhere else. But if you could watch coaches' film, you would see running backs, wide receivers, and tight ends coming across and knocking the umpire down. But if the ball is thrown deep, your eyes and the camera follow the ball and you never see what happens to the umpire.

I think full-time officials, younger officials, instant replay, the whole thing has to be redone. And when they put in a rule, make sure it can be officiated with consistency.

But if the NFL is ever going to solve its officiating problem, the program has to carry over into the off-season. Someone once said that a tragedy has only a ten-day life for other people, then it's forgotten. I think a bad call has only a ten-day life. Even then, it's all over by February.

For the NFL to do something, it's going to take a bad call that carries over into the off-season. Maybe a bad call in the Super Bowl that lets the wrong team win, a bad call that's not forgotten in ten days.

OTHER THOUGHTS ON OTHER SPORTS

I'm always meeting people who ask me why I don't do other sports on television, why I just do football. My answer is that I'm not a television guy, I'm a football guy. I don't want to be what I'm not.

I know football, but I don't know enough about other sports to be a television analyst. I'm a fan of most other sports. But that's different from knowing other sports well enough to be an analyst. If you're talking about why things are happening in a sport, you better know what you're talking about. If you don't, you're not credible.

Of all the other sports on television, I probably watch boxing the most. I know boxing well enough to interview fighters, like I did Marvelous Marvin Hagler and Ray Mancini a few years ago for CBS and the Fox interview with Mike Tyson that was shown before his 1995 fight with Buster Mathis Jr. But that day Mike was asking me questions too.

"How fast does your bus go?" he said.

I told him I really didn't know, that my drivers, Willie and Dave, stay right at the speed limit. I guessed eighty-five would be about the top speed, but of all the people who have ever asked me about my bus, Mike was the first to ask how fast it went. He asked me about football too, but when I asked him if he ever played football, he laughed.

"Football is too violent for me," he said. "I couldn't stand having somebody hitting me from behind. That's the thing about boxing. Everything is always in front of you."

I know boxing well enough to talk about it with Mike Tyson, but I don't know boxing like Gil Clancy does. Long before he was a television analyst, Gil was a boxing trainer. He had dozens of fighters, including George Foreman and Emile Griffith. He knows boxing from the inside. I know it as a fan. There's a difference, a big enough difference for me to know that I couldn't do what Gil does. I wouldn't be a credible boxing analyst.

But as a fan and as a guy who played other sports as a kid, I can relate to other sports and to athletes in those sports.

One of Mickey Mantle's closest friends in Dallas was Pat Summerall; and when Mickey died, I remembered Pat telling how in Mickey's later years he had one recurring dream. He hit the ball into the outfield for what should have been a single or a double, but he'd get thrown out at first base. He couldn't run anymore. And he had once been one of the fastest players in baseball.

Hey, as a kid I could run too; but as a catcher at Jefferson Union High School, I looked at baseball from the backside of life.

When you're a catcher, you're the one guy who faces everybody else on your team. Your teammates have their backs to the fences and they're looking in, but as the catcher you have your back to the crowd and you're looking out. We're kind of a fraternity, catchers. If you were a catcher, you couldn't picture yourself as an outfielder like Mickey Mantle unless it was batting practice and you were out there hanging out so you wouldn't have to warm up pitchers. I hated warming up pitchers. They'd throw the ball as hard as they could and you had to catch it. I hated catching batting practice too. I'd always get hit with foul tips.

But an outfielder, that was different. That had to be fun. That's why I understood what Michael Jordan was doing when he decided to play baseball in 1994 for the Chicago White Sox's farm team in Birmingham.

Most people couldn't figure it out. He had stopped playing basketball for the Chicago Bulls, and now he was playing Minor League baseball. Hey, he's a human being. How many people do you know, if they had a chance to take a year off and go play Minor League baseball, would go do it. I know guys that are doctors and lawyers, they pay big money to go to these baseball fantasy camps. To me, that's what Michael Jordan was doing. He was anybody who ever thought, *Hey, if I could go on the golf tour for a year, I'd quit what I do and go do it. Or if I could sing on the stage for a year, I'd go do it.* Just wishing you could do something you always wanted to do and go do it. Maybe I'm goofy, but I think with most people that thought is more normal than not.

Most guys, if they could afford to quit their jobs and go play a year of Minor League baseball and travel around in their own bus, they'd do it just for the fun of it. To me, it's a very normal thought process, and Michael Jordan was able to do it because he had the dough.

Maybe professional sports have become so much about business, we can't say just look at the fun. Some people like to go up in the woods and sleep in tents, go hiking in the mountains, paddle a kayak, or go bungee jumping. They do it for the fun of it.

I think Michael would have preferred to play golf on the PGA Tour, but he realized that was harder even than playing baseball. Hitting that stupid little ball that's standing still and hitting it straight and far and trying to putt it into a hole that's four and one-quarter inches wide can be harder than hitting a fastball or a curveball. Michael found that out. So has everybody who has ever played golf.

But when I play, I use what I call the FIDO theory. If you hit a bad one, you Forget It and Drive On.

If I hit a bad one, my son Mike or somebody else goes and gets that ball, then I hit another one. By not going to get the bad one, I don't even remember it. If you have to walk and chase the bad ones, then you remember 'em. But if you never have to go in the creeks and lakes and trees and bushes and stuff, then you don't think you played poorly. My way, I always have a good lie. I'm always where I should be. But sometimes I'll use close to a dozen balls in nine holes.

Back when I did those Miller Lite commercials, I got freebie balls with a Miller Lite logo. I'd hit 'em in people's backyards and swimming pools and down their chimneys, and as soon as they saw the logo, they thought I had hit it there. They were right, except that Billy Martin lived near me for a while, and he used those Miller Lite balls, so if anybody said anything to me, I'd always blame Billy.

"No, no," I'd tell them. "I haven't played that hole near your house. Must've been Billy."

But after Billy moved, people knew it had to be me. Then when Miller Lite stopped sending me those balls, they couldn't blame me anymore. One time I played with a guy who was so bad, he quit on the first hole. He hit his tee shot out of bounds, then he hit another tee shot out of bounds. He motioned for me to hit my tee shot, then he said, "I'll put a ball down by yours." Then he hit that one out of bounds. He dropped another, but dribbled that one into a trap. His shot out of the trap flew over the green and almost hit some people. When they yelled at him, he got into his cart and went home. When the going got tough, he just quit. But here I was out there by myself. Another guy came along and asked me, "What's with him?"

"He said he was hurt," I told him, "but the only thing hurt was his feelings."

That's why I approach golf the way I do. I don't care. When you don't care, you never get upset. Most people, they hit a bad shot, they moan or groan. But if you don't care, if you use the FIDO theory when you hit a ball into the woods or a pond, you just put another ball down and hit it. And don't look for the first ball.

If you've ever looked at a golf pro's irons, you'll see a worn spot in the middle of the club. My irons have marks on the toe of the club.

You wouldn't think you could do that. If you were to take a swing at a golf ball with, say, a 5-iron, it would make sense that you're going to hit it in the middle of the club. That's the easiest place to hit it. And if you were to judge hitting a golf ball by the degree of difficulty, like in diving or figure skating, if you had to hit it on the toe, or tip, of the club, that would be the most difficult thing to do. But if you're a bad golfer, that's the easiest thing to do.

That's why golf is so frustrating. You're out there all by yourself. If you hit a bad shot, there's no one else to blame.

In football or baseball or basketball, you can always say, "Hey, I played good but those other guys were lousy." In football, you've got maybe thirty-five other guys you can blame. In baseball, eight or nine other guys. In basketball, four other guys. Or if you're a coach or a general manager, you can always say, "My players didn't play good." In tennis, you can blame the linesmen. In boxing, if you lose a decision, you can always blame the judges.

Being out there all by yourself in golf, maybe that's why people figure they have to say something after every shot. You'll hear, "That'll play," which means it was awful. Or you'll hear the other guy say, "Too bad," which means he's really not sorry you're in the water. Or you'll hear people talking to the ball, saying "Jump . . . Run . . . Bite . . . Stop." But the ball can't hear you or talk back to you. Yet everybody talks to the ball.

That's because we all have stupid genes in us, and golf brings out those stupid genes.

If you put a golf ball on a table in your home, you'd never talk to it. You'd never say, "Run" or "Come back." But out on a golf course, you're talking to that ball all the time. You talk to the other guy's ball too. But you only do it out on the golf course. You take that same ball that you give so much attention to, if you put it in your car, if you put it where you work, put it anyplace else, you'd never talk to that ball. But when you're out there on a golf course, you'll talk to it.

Talk about someone that should feel they're wanted only some of the time, that's a golf ball. Out on the golf course, you get a lot of attention. Off the course, no one even talks to you.

Another thing that brings out those stupid genes is the clothes golfers wear. Guys will wear plaid slacks or what they call knickers—they wouldn't wear them anywhere else. They certainly wouldn't wear them walking down Market Street in San Francisco or Michigan Avenue in Chicago or Wall Street in New York. Yet they'll go out on a golf course and wear them. So golf brings out what you wear and how you talk. Golf brings out the stupid genes in all of us.

But no matter what golf pros wear or say, they can't have too many stupid genes. I realized that when I watched their practice rounds before the 1992 U.S. Open at Pebble Beach.

The pros would go to the range to hit their woods and irons, but during their practice rounds out on the course, that's when they really practiced their chipping and putting. After each hole, they dropped a bunch of balls around the green, some in the rough, some in the sand traps. It looked like an Easter egg hunt. Then they chipped those balls out of the rough or blasted them out of the sand. Then they putted for a few minutes. But they didn't putt to where the hole was that day. They putted to the four different areas of the green where they knew the holes would be cut during the Open's four rounds.

The golf pros I've met, I really like. They're good guys. Especially Davis Love III, who is really skinny at six feet three and 175 but is one of the great eaters.

I always thought Ben Davidson, one of my Raiders defensive ends, was the biggest eater I'd ever seen. At dinner in training camp Ben would eat for an hour and a half. Three or four steaks. But Davis is right up there. He'll order a big steak for himself and chicken for his wife and daughter, then he'll finish whatever anybody else doesn't eat. For dessert he'll order, say, chocolate cake for himself and apple pie, cookies, and ice cream "for the table." Hey, he's the table. His father, Davis Love Jr., once played the PGA Tour and later was a great teaching pro. Davis is a teacher too. When he and Michael Jordan were together at the University of North Carolina, he got Michael started playing golf when everybody else thought of Michael only as a basketball player, long before Michael was on all these television commercials for sneakers and hamburgers and everything else. But as great as Michael has been for the National Basketball Association and for basketball itself, sometimes you worry about the fundamentals of the sport.

Michael made the dunk dramatic. And when you can put a word like that on it, *dunk,* it makes it easier for people to get excited about it. Dunk is like home run in baseball, bomb in football, knockout in boxing. But nobody in basketball has a word for a good pass or for a guy who handles the ball well or someone who just makes a regular shot. Nobody gets excited about fundamentals. They get excited about the extraordinary, not the ordinary, because the extraordinary has a name. They make television commercials about it. And it's on all the television highlights. So every kid wants to do it. If they're in the eighth grade, they've got a low basket in their backyard and they're out there dunking. But they're not out there learning to pass or learning to handle the ball or learning to shoot.

It's the same with defense. Not enough people give credit to a team playing good defense. On television, we're used to seeing too many games through the eyes of the offense. It's always the offensive team that has missed, say, ten straight shots. It's always the offensive team that's cold instead of crediting the defensive team for making them miss those shots.

When college basketball gets to its NCAA tournament, I don't like the way television jumps around among the early-round games. Their theory is to try to satisfy everyone, but usually they don't satisfy anyone. When they jump around from here to there, back and forth, you don't know what you're watching. By the time I really get into a game, then go to the refrigerator and come back, another game is on. You're watching different teams and you're hearing different voices. So you try to get into that game, but by the time you do, they say, "Now we're taking you to Wisconsin Green Bay." When I first heard that, I thought they had it backward, that they were really going to Green Bay, Wisconsin, where I go to see the Packers play.

You never put the state before the city. You learn that in second-grade geography. But sure enough they meant Wisconsin Green Bay, which is really the University of Wisconsin at Green Bay.

Another thing about basketball that annoys me is all those time-outs at the end of a game. Two or three coaches in suits are talking, but there are only five players listening, and maybe not all of them. The head coach is drawing a play on his clipboard. When he does that, I always figure this will be a great play. Once when the New York Knicks came back on the court after a time-out I expected a great play, but they whipped the ball around and threw it out of bounds. They took a time-out to draw that play.

But at least the NBA players admit they're pros. Too many college players are really pros too. They're there to play basketball or football, not to study or go to class.

Sure, some study and go to class and are real student-athletes. But too many don't, and they ought to admit it. That's the hypocrisy at too many colleges. Because of the pressure to go to the NCAA tournament or to bowl games in order to make money for the school, the pressure is on the coach to win. So to win, he has to recruit the best players, who may not be the best students. Once he gets those players, he has to do whatever he can to keep them in school even though they don't have much time to study or go to class because they have too many games to play to make money for the school.

The NCAA also lets its basketball tournament go on too long. The last few years, the championship game has been played on the first Monday of April, a few hours after baseball's opening-day games when some celebrity or politician throws out the first ball. Usually badly.

If you're going to throw out the first ball, I think you owe it to yourself and to the crowd at the ballpark to practice it. To just go out there and short-arm it and to see the ball plop into the dirt halfway to home plate, why bother? You've got to lengthen your arm out. If I ever threw out the first ball, I'd throw it as far as I could. If anything, it'd go over the catcher's head. The best first-ball thrower I've seen lately was Cindy Crawford, the model. She got out there on the mound and threw some heat. She wound up and *whoom,* let that thing fly. I figured she'd throw it dainty and bounce it. She wound up and flung it. Of all the people throwing out the first ball, including the President, she was the best I've seen.

But nobody should be throwing out the first ball of the baseball season in April when March Madness is ending that night. Sports are being piled on top of each other like dirty clothes.

Hey, the NBA finals and hockey's Stanley Cup finals end in mid-June now. No wonder most teams have had trouble repeating as champions. By the time the two teams in the finals finish, it's only three months until the National Hockey League teams go to training camp, only four until the NBA teams do. That's not much time for their bodies to recoup.

I've never really appreciated hockey, but that's my fault. Until a few days into 1996, I had never gone to a hockey game. While waiting for the NFC championship game in Dallas, my son Mike and I went to see one of Wayne Gretzky's last games for the Los Angeles Kings. As good as the action was, what went on in the penalty box right below us was even better.

The penalty-box timekeeper, an NHL official in a business suit, had three water bottles, one each for the referee and the two linesmen to use during a stoppage in play. He also had a bucket of ice with pucks in it. The ice kept the pucks frozen so they wouldn't bounce.

But every time a player clomped into the box to serve his penalty, the first thing he did was drink out of one of the water bottles when the timekeeper wasn't looking, then spit into the ice bucket where the frozen pucks were.

Now that I've finally seen a hockey game live, I have a little better idea of what goes on; but if I'm watching a game on television, I hear fans yelling but I still don't always know what they're yelling about. Crossing one of those lines. Icing, whatever that is. I never know when to yell or when to keep quiet. If you're trying to watch a hockey game on television and you've never gone to a game, you might know who to root for, but you don't know when.

I didn't grow up with hockey. I never thought I'd see the day when the San Jose Sharks would be the lead story on the San Francisco sports pages. But when the Sharks upset the Detroit Red Wings in the 1994 playoffs, they had the biggest headlines. And whenever Wayne Gretzky did something big, he always got a big headline, but I understood that.

On their way to greatness, some people aren't always nice guys all the time, but Wayne Gretzky is just a great guy. That's what makes what he's done all the more meaningful. He's just a nice person. You could tell that the night he broke Gordie Howe's record for goals. When they stopped the game to give him the puck and take all the pictures, the first thing he did was thank Vancouver for allowing this to happen there. Now that's a thoughtful person. But when you see him dressed up, there's not much to him. When you think of hockey, you think of big strong tough guys. When you look at Gretzky, you wonder, where's the stuff that makes all these goals and assists happen? As slender as he is, the goons never could catch him. He's always been too quick and too good.

As a kid, I ice-skated in Winterland but I never played hockey. In our neighborhood in Daly City across the San Francisco line, we didn't go out and slap the puck around. Even when I ice-skated, I never thought about playing hockey. I was too busy trying to keep my skates from going out while my ankles were going in. Other people glided around. I didn't. Roller-skating and riding a bicycle, they came natural, but ice-skating didn't come natural to this guy. Skates out, ankles in, and hold on to that rail. That's what amazes me about figure skaters, the things they can do on those skates. When you've tried it and you can't even stand on skates, then see the things those figure skaters do, they're just amazing.

Another thing is, they can go full speed, sweat, get tired, and still smile while they're skating. That's a hard thing to do. Working hard, sweating, and smiling usually don't go together.

To me, figure skating is like dancing. It's an art, not a sport. Not that dancers and figure skaters aren't athletes, but what they do isn't sports. What Bonnie Blair and Dan Jansen do as speed skaters is sports. Especially in the Olympics where your timing has to be just right. If you're not right that day, you have to wait until the next Olympics. When Dan fell twice in Calgary in 1988 and then didn't do well in Albertville in 1992, some people started to believe that the Olympics made him choke. I was glad to see him win the 1,000-meter gold medal at Lillehammer, just to knock that stuff off.

The Olympics were for so-called amateurs for so long that some people still don't like to see our NBA players in the Olympics, but when we'd get beaten by the Soviets in basketball, like we did in 1972 and 1988, their amateurs were really pros. We were depending on college players to go against these Soviet players who were training full-time and getting paid by the Soviet government. The purity of "amateurs" in many sports (track and field, hockey, skiing) hasn't existed for many years. So if you admit that, our Olympic team might as well use the players who get paid the most, the NBA players.

Even with the pros, the Olympics are still a great spectacle, but soccer's World Cup is a great party. When the World Cup was held in the United States in 1994, it was a festival.

Outside and inside the stadiums, people played music, danced, and drank beer. You don't see that festive mood at football games or basketball games or baseball games. But those soccer fans, they showed up festive. They were celebrating before the game started. I learned why soccer is the world's most popular sport. It's not a game, it's a party.

The people just use the soccer game as a backdrop for the party.

The day Cameroon played—I'm probably just showing how stupid I am—but I didn't know where Cameroon is or what Cameroon is. I learned later that it's a country on Africa's western coast. But did I miss something? Did it used to go by another name?

Here was this big game, Brazil against Cameroon, and I'd never heard of Cameroon. Because I don't fly, I don't get to many other countries. Canada and Mexico are as far as I've gone. I still remember my geography but I don't think there was a Cameroon when I was a kid. I know the names of countries change, so some country that was whatever then might be Cameroon now. I know there's a Brazil, there's always been a Brazil with Brazilians, but what would the people in Cameroon be—Cameroonians? How many Cameroonians can there be? How many people would wear a Cameroonian cap? But at that soccer game there were thousands of people wearing those caps and having a party and I enjoyed watching it even though I didn't really understand it.

Another thing I don't understand is the weight they put on racehorses. They're always so concerned about weight. The weight of the jockey, the weight in the saddle. You can't be a pound here and there. The weight is so important. But no one ever has any idea what the horse weighs. How can the stewards be so concerned about how much weight is on top of the horse without knowing what the horse weighs?

Athletes have their best weights. An athlete can be too heavy or too light to perform well. I don't know why horses would be any different. The trainer probably knows how much the horse weighs, or should weigh, but it's never mentioned. Racetrack guys will tell you the exact weight on top of the horse, but no one ever mentions how much the horse weighs.

Maybe that's just part of the mystery. You can always tell if a racetrack guy is knowledgeable if he talks out of the side of his mouth. At a racetrack, always listen to those guys. All those guys who talk straight, they don't know anything. But if it comes out of the side of somebody's mouth, it's a lot more fun to listen to.

ON THE BUS WITH WILLIE AND DAVE

Every so often in my travels, people I meet along the way will ask if they can see what the inside of my bus looks like. Almost all of them have the same request.

"I want to see the table where the turkey is on Thanksgiving," they'll say. "The six-legged turkey."

When I started giving "Turkey Leg" awards in 1989 to players in our Thanksgiving Day game, we had a regular two-legged turkey and Reggie White, who was then with the Eagles, got both of them. But year by year, we had to get more turkeys so we could award more turkey legs. In 1992, we needed six for Emmitt Smith and the Cowboys' offensive linemen. Now we always set up an eight-legged turkey on the table in the bus. The bigger the turkey, the more legs it needs. That's simple anatomy.

Hey, it's Thanksgiving, it's turkey, it's football, it's tradition.

To me, Thanksgiving has always been a football tradition more than a family tradition. When I was on the Jefferson Union High School team in Daly City, we always played South City on Thanksgiving Day. When I was in college at the University of Oregon, Grays Harbor (in

Aberdeen, Washington), and Cal Poly (in San Luis Obispo, California), I was always away on Thanksgiving Day, usually getting ready to play a game that Saturday. When I was coaching at Hancock College, Cal Poly, and San Diego State, the same thing. When I was coaching the Raiders, we always practiced Thanksgiving morning. And ever since 1981, I've been broadcasting an NFL game on Thanksgiving either in Dallas or in Detroit.

You always try to make a Thanksgiving Day out of wherever you are. In Dallas or Detroit, we have a big Thanksgiving party in our hotel on Wednesday night before the game for all our production guys and technical guys, the game officials, and the Cowboys' or Lions' public relations guys, whoever wants to come.

After we get to Texas Stadium or the Silverdome for the game, our guys sit around and have some turkey. We usually have about six turkeys. Pat Summerall always brings a smoked turkey. One time in Dallas we even had a deep-fried turkey. You shoot jalapeño sauce into it, then deep-fry it. After the game some people stop by again, then when the bus starts moving, there's another turkey for whoever is traveling with us to our Sunday game.

My customized bus, now called the Outback Steakhouse Madden Cruiser, can seat ten in big chairs, a long couch, and a booth-with-a-table that breaks down into a sleeper bunk. It has three TV sets with a Sony DSS Satellite System and four phones. It has a refrigerator, a microwave oven, and a sink. In the back, my big bed is almost the width of the bus. It has a stall shower with a sink and a flush toilet. Two former Greyhound drivers, Willie Yarborough and Dave Hahn, share the wheel.

"All the years Willie and I have been driving," Dave likes to say, "John has never been late for anything."

It's like I told Mike Tyson, I really don't know how fast my bus goes because Willie and Dave stay right at the speed limit. But in Texas one night Willie was rolling along when he noticed a highway patrol car's red lights flashing behind him.

"Uh-oh," Willie said, "I think we're going to get our first ticket."

"What do you mean *we?*" I said. "There's only one driver here."

It turned out that Willie hadn't noticed a slow-down sign for construction, but the highway patrolman just gave us a warning.

I mean, he gave Willie a warning.

For me, the bus is the perfect way to travel. When I was coaching, I didn't like to fly, but I did it because I had to. Whenever the seat-belt sign flashed on, my stomach flashed on. But on the Raiders' charter, I could get up and walk around more than I could on a regular commercial flight. Being in that big tube wasn't so claustrophobic. But when I started doing games for CBS, I had to take commercial flights. After doing a Packers–Bucs game in Tampa the Sunday after Thanksgiving in 1979, I boarded a flight to San Francisco with a stop in Houston. I'd been woozy on some previous flights that season, but this was the worst. When the plane stopped in Houston, I got off and called my wife, Virginia. As always, she understood.

"I'm taking the train to Los Angeles," I told her.

"I'll drive down there and pick you up," she said.

That's the last time I've been on a plane. I rode Amtrak trains to games until I got my first bus in 1987. Years ago, I read John Steinbeck's *Travels with Charley,* a great book about driving all over the United States in a camper with his bluish-gray French poodle. I thought, *What a great way to see and know this country.* That's what I've been able to do on my bus. I've crossed the Mississippi on maybe ten different bridges. I've stopped to buy sweet corn in Illinois right out of the cornfield. I've ice-fished in a Minnesota lake. I've had alligator stew with the Boudreau brothers in Louisiana. I've ridden for miles in Wyoming and Texas without seeing a house. I've stayed in all the big cities.

Beginning with Fox's first preseason game, I'm in hotels or on the bus the rest of the season except for going home to Danville, California, to do a San Francisco game every so often. But everywhere I go, when people ask me who I think will win Sunday's game, I always say the home team. If the game is in Dallas, I like the Cowboys. If the game's in Green Bay, I like the Packers.

I've never been a gourmet. I don't go out to dine. I go out to eat. On the bus, we usually get off the interstate and go into a town to find a nice place, but not a fancy place. Once in a while we eat in a truck stop where the menu will always include chicken-fried steak. You can go into any truck stop off any interstate for breakfast, lunch, or dinner, any time of day or night, and chicken-fried steak will be on the menu.

Of all the cities, Dallas seems to bring out the best in one of my favorite traveling subjects. Food.

When Tony Casillas was a defensive tackle for the Cowboys, his friend Mico Rodriguez had a Mexican restaurant chain, Mi Cocina, that served great tamales. I love tamales. One Saturday when I was there for a game, I walked into the Cowboys' locker room at Valley Ranch and there were all these tamales. Hundreds of 'em with all the hot sauces. I started eating and I couldn't stop. I had tamale after tamale after tamale. The next day I mentioned the tamales on the air.

"I could eat fifty tamales," I said.

Some people didn't believe me. Other people started sending me tamales. Another time when I had back-to-back games in Dallas, the Cowboys' public-relations director, Rich Dalrymple, invited me to the Thursday dinner the Cowboys have for their quarterbacks and coaches and their wives. I was sitting with Troy Aikman and Jason Garrett when they started talking about who was going to pick up the Stubbs the next morning.

"I'll pay for 'em," Troy said. "Do me a favor and pick 'em up."

"I've got other stops," Jason said. "I can't pick up the Stubbs."

"What's the Stubbs?" I said. "What are you guys talking about?"

One of their defensive ends, Daniel Stubbs, came to their Valley Ranch complex every day with this huge sandwich from the Coppell Deli—two fried eggs, sausage, bacon, and cheese on Texas toast. The deli owner, Jay Khorrami, put it up on the board there as the "Stubbs" for $2.49. Pretty soon other players were stopping and ordering a Stubbs to go. It became a team thing. When we stopped by the Cowboys' practice on Saturday to talk to the players and coaches, Troy walked into our meeting with a stack of Stubbses for us. We ate some, put the leftovers in the refrigerator on the bus, and heated them in the microwave later. On the All-Madden team that year, the Stubbs was my All-Madden sandwich.

Don't ask me about its cholesterol and fat numbers. When we took it down to the Pritikin Longevity Center in Santa Monica, one of their doctors, Jay Kenney, wouldn't even touch it. He used tongs to pick it up. "It's got more saturated fat and cholesterol," he said, "than just about anything we've ever analyzed here." He wouldn't even touch it, much less eat it. We never did get the fat and cholesterol numbers. Probably just as well. But it tastes great.

When you're on the road as much as I am, you look forward to those taste treats. Whenever we go to Green Bay for a game, we always stop in Chili John's across from where the Northland Hotel used to be. For years the Northland was Green Bay's only major hotel. Whenever an NFL team went there to play the Packers, they stayed there. Right across the street was Chili John's with its specialty of chili over beans or spaghetti. Chili John's is out in a mall now but when we're in Green Bay, we'll get some to go and eat it while we're watching Packer tapes.

Green Bay is one of my favorite stops. There's just something about the town and Lambeau Field, especially in November or December when it's cold and the bratwurst is cooking on the grills in the parking lot. It's even better if it's snowing. That to me is what pro football is all about. That's where the NFL started, in towns like Green Bay and Canton, Ohio, where the Pro Football Hall of Fame is now.

Whenever I'm in Green Bay it always makes me think that if it weren't for what Curly Lambeau and the original Packers did there in the 1920s, maybe none of us in pro football now would be doing what we're doing, maybe there wouldn't be any fans wearing those foam-rubber cheeseheads in the stands there. Everybody laughs when they see somebody wearing a cheesehead, but hey, one of those foam-rubber cheeseheads saved a guy's life. Coming home after wearing his cheesehead at a Packers game in Cleveland late in the 1995 season, Frank Emmert Jr., an aerial photographer from Superior, Wisconsin, was in a Cessna 172 that suddenly lost power and crashed.

"I put my cheesehead in front of me," he said later. "Everyone's been saying they can't believe I'm alive."

He had a shattered right ankle, cuts, and bruises, but his cheesehead let him live to go to Lambeau Field again.

Hey, if all the NFL games could be played in one stadium, Lambeau Field would be the perfect place. You can get caught up in all these fancy stadiums and luxury suites and you may think that's what pro football is, but then you go to Green Bay, Wisconsin, and you realize this is what pro football really is. Even with luxury suites, Lambeau Field still has the great look of an old stadium. If you close your eyes, you can still see Vince Lombardi walking the sideline in his brown fedora and camel's hair coat.

Soldier Field in Chicago has that same ol' pro football atmosphere. The entire NFC Central once had that feeling when the Vikings were in Metropolitan Stadium out there in what is now one of the world's largest malls, in Bloomington near Minneapolis, and when the Lions were in Tiger Stadium in downtown Detroit—the ol' black-and-blue division. But now the Vikings are in the Metrodome, the Lions are in the Silverdome, and Tampa Bay might as well be in a dome. All you have left is Lambeau Field and Soldier Field.

I know the Bears used to play at Wrigley Field but Soldier Field down near Lake Michigan still gives me the feel of George Halas and the "Monsters of the Midway" back in the 1940s. For years one of the greatest Bears ever, Dick Butkus, did radio there. Chicago is just a good place to be. I love to walk Michigan Avenue at night in either direction. It's just the greatest walk there is, especially at Christmas time.

The Chicago newspapers are always filled with stories about the Bears, and there are sports radio talk shows, sports TV shows. Everybody there knows the Bears, everybody knows pro football and "Bears" is still pro football's best nickname. Some nicknames in sports now, like the Colorado Rockies, is that baseball or hockey? But when somebody talks about the Bears, you don't say, "Is that the basketball team?" *Bears* is the perfect nickname for a pro football team, even better than Giants. Bears means big guys, it means pro football. And the Bears have lived up to that nickname.

Whenever I'm in Chicago, I go to the Billy Goat Tavern and Grill on North Michigan Avenue's lower level, down where the trucks unload, the place John Belushi and Dan Aykroyd made famous on their *Saturday Night Live* skits. It's not fancy, but that's why it's my kind of place.

I've had an apartment in New York for more than ten years, but I've never been to what you would call fancy restaurants. They probably wouldn't let me in anyway, not in my windbreaker and sneakers. But there are plenty of great little restaurants. In the morning I'll read all the papers in a coffee shop, then I'll sit on a bench in Central Park and watch people come and go or take a walk. Some recognize me, but they're moving so fast, they just say, "Hey, John, how you doing?" and keep going.

Another good walking town is New Orleans, but only when it's quiet. One year we did a wild-card game there on New Year's Eve, the night before the Sugar Bowl, but the French Quarter was just too wild to walk around.

All the times I've been in Washington for Redskins games, I've been ashamed of myself for not going to the Smithsonian or the Washington Monument, the Lincoln Memorial or the Jefferson Memorial. I'm embarrassed to say I really wouldn't know one of those places from another. Washington is our nation's capital and there's so much there. People come from all over the world to go there. I'm usually there two or three times a season, but I've never been to the White House or anyplace else. Every time I think about it, I'm embarrassed. We usually get to our hotel there on Friday night, go to Redskin Park way out in Virginia on Saturday, get back late, have our production meeting in the hotel, go to bed, get up, go to RFK Stadium, do the game, get on the bus and leave.

RFK is another of my favorite stadiums. It's old but it's great. When the Redskins get those fans stomping their feet, RFK actually shakes. In our booth, you can feel the stadium moving. Even our cameras move.

When the Eagles are rolling, Veterans Stadium in Philadelphia also shakes a little. But the best thing in Philadelphia for me is its cheesesteaks. Thinly sliced steak and onions with a cheese sauce. But they don't travel well. Buy one at a stand in South Philly and eat it right there, hot off the grill. If it's wrapped up and carried, it's not the same. Another favorite of mine, Buffalo chicken wings, travel much better, especially if they're from the Anchor Bar in Buffalo where they originated.

In the early years of the American Football League, the Anchor Bar was near old War Memorial Stadium where the Bills played and practiced.

"After our morning meetings," Paul Maguire told me, "some of us would go to the Anchor for wings and beer, then practice in the afternoon."

Kansas City is another good food town. I learned to appreciate it when I was coaching the Raiders and we played there every season. When our plane landed (I flew in those years), everyone would go to Gates Barbecue, one of the best barbecues in the world. There was only one Gates place then, but now they're all over town. I always bring back some Gates sauce. That love of barbecue is why Kansas City is one of the best tailgate scenes. It's almost a college scene. Most people wear something with Chiefs red in it and they're always there early. Being a great barbecue town and a great beef town, they know how to do it. During a game there in 1995 we showed some videotape of some good barbecue cooking in the parking lot, then we showed a fancy chocolate dessert with raspberry sauce and a lemon wedge.

"The heck with that squirt stuff and lemon," I said.

The next week, I got a letter and a box of chocolate and squirt stuff from a Kansas City lady, a professional caterer, defending her squirt stuff. She got after me in a nice way. As an apology, we showed her squirt stuff again. I'm sure it's good, if you like that sort of stuff. But there's another thing about Kansas City fans that I like. They not only know how to make a lot of noise, they know when to make noise, like when the other team has the ball.

As much as I enjoy Kansas City, I seldom get there. Under the Fox contract, the visiting team is always an NFC team. So for me to get to an AFC city, an NFC team has to play an important game there. The way the schedule has fallen, I haven't been in Denver lately. I've seldom done games in New England, Indianapolis, and Miami (where we stayed at the Don Shula Motel in Miami Lakes).

When I was in the restaurant, I asked the waitress, "Does Don cook all this stuff? Is this his recipe?"

When I was walking through the lobby, I pointed to a painting on the wall and asked a bellboy, "Did Don do that?"

When the chambermaid was making up my bed, I asked her, "Does Don check these rooms after you clean 'em?"

When I go to Pittsburgh, I don't make jokes. To me, there's nothing funny about Pittsburgh. That's where the Steelers knocked my Raiders' team out of the AFC playoffs in 1972 on Franco Harris's Immaculate Reception. I still get mad every time I think about it. We were leading, 7–6, with twenty seconds left. Steelers' ball, fourth and ten at their 40-yard line. At the snap, our pass rush pressured Terry Bradshaw into scrambling and throwing a desperation pass to Frenchy Fuqua as our safety, Jack Tatum, went for the ball. It bounced off one of them (even after all the films I've seen, I'm still not sure which one) and floated toward Franco Harris, who reached down, caught it at full speed at our 42 and ran untouched into the end zone with five seconds showing on the clock.

But none of the officials immediately raised his arms to signal a touchdown.

Under today's rules, it wouldn't have made any difference which player the ball bounced off. But at the time the rules were different. If it bounced off an offensive player (Fuqua), a teammate was ineligible to catch it. If it bounced off a defensive player (Tatum), then Franco Harris was eligible to catch it.

After the officials huddled in the end zone, the referee, Fred Swearingen, hurried to the phone in one of the nearby baseball dugouts.

I learned later that Swearingen called Art McNally, the NFL's supervisor of officials, who was sitting near a TV monitor in the press box with Jim Kensil, then the NFL's executive director. Because of the TV monitor, Art was accused of having used instant replay to determine whether the ball bounced off Fuqua or Tatum, but Art always denied that.

This, remember, was 1972, fourteen years before the NFL adopted instant replay to help its officials.

Art's explanation has always been that, because the play would virtually decide a playoff game, Swearingen wanted to be sure of the rule. Whatever their conversation was about, after at least thirty seconds, a long, long time when you're waiting for a decision to decide a playoff game, Swearingen hopped out of the dugout and raised his arms. Touchdown.

We had time for one play, a long pass from Kenny Stabler to Raymond Chester that the Steelers broke up. We lost, 13–7. We were out of the playoffs.

Of all my losing games, that was the most depressing, the most confusing, the most mysterious. If the officials knew it was a touchdown, why didn't they call it a touchdown immediately? If they didn't know it was a touchdown, how did they discover it was? From checking with Art McNally who was sitting near a TV monitor where the instant replay was being shown?

Now you know why I don't make jokes in Pittsburgh. Nearly fifteen years later, the day before we did a Giants–Steelers preseason game there in 1987, I was out on the field at Three Rivers Stadium watching the Steelers practice, when I turned to Bob Stenner and pointed to the first-base dugout.

"See that phone on the wall," I said. "That's the phone Fred Swearingen used."

Walking through that dugout on our way off the field that day, Bob ripped the phone off the wall and tossed it in his briefcase.

"Here, John," he said later, "this is for you."

I had the phone mounted as a trophy. I still have it.

Back when Chuck Noll was coaching the Steelers, I always thought about the Immaculate Reception whenever I went to Pittsburgh to do a game. But it doesn't bug me like it used to. Bill Cowher is the coach now. The players are all different. Art Rooney's son Dan, the Steelers' president, doesn't even bring it up anymore. Hey, the play happened a generation ago. Some of the fans don't know much about it except what they've been told or read. It's lived its life.

But it's still a mystery to me. It always will be.

Another mystery to me is how the seagulls always perch on the roof or in the rafters at Candlestick Park when a 49ers game is winding down. Whenever I mention that, guys will always tell me, "It's the food." Hey, the food is there during the pregame warm-up but the seagulls aren't flying around. The food is there during the game, but the seagulls aren't there. They just sit on the roof or in the rafters until the last two minutes of the game.

How do they know the game's about to end? How do they know to gather at Candlestick when their ancestors never gathered at Kezar Stadium where I grew up watching the 49ers?

Maybe the seagulls knew there wouldn't be much food in the parking lot at Kezar because there wasn't any parking lot. Everybody talks now about how a stadium needs all this parking, but Kezar didn't have a parking lot. If you had a car, you parked somewhere on the street out there near Golden Gate Park and started walking.

But in all my travels, there's one memory that won't go away.

I like to go to Dallas to see the Cowboys, but whenever I'm there, somebody who doesn't know me that well will suggest going to the Book Depository where Lee Harvey Oswald was hiding when he shot John F. Kennedy.

"You can go there if you want to," I always say, "but I've never gone there and I never will."

I'm not saying anybody who does go there is wrong because everybody's different, but I won't go there. Maybe it's because to me, John F. Kennedy was the last President who was really a President and Jacqueline Kennedy was the last First Lady who was really a person. Maybe it's my age. I was twenty-seven then. I had grown up in a time when being the President of the United States meant more than it does now. As a kid, I remembered President Roosevelt and President Truman and President Eisenhower. They represented authority.

So did Mr. John Mongon, the assistant principal at Jefferson Union High School. So did Sister Superior at my grade school, Our Lady of Perpetual Help in Daly City across the San Francisco city line. I never knew that nun's name. She was just Sister Superior. If she even looked at me, I was terrified.

That November day in 1963 when John F. Kennedy was assassinated in Dallas, I was a coach at Hancock Junior College in Santa Maria on the California coast. I was in my office when I heard about it. CNN didn't exist then. You got news in bits and pieces on the radio. Later in the day I watched television and I can still see Mrs. Kennedy getting off *Air Force One* with the President's body.

I couldn't believe it all happened. I still can't.

IN THE BOOTH
WITH PAT

In preparing to do a game, I always come across stories I can use on the air. Like the one about Mickey Marvin and the batteries.

Mickey is a big rosy-cheeked guy who's now a Raiders scout, but this happened when he was a Raiders guard. About two hours before a 1981 game he was getting his ankles taped while just wearing his jockstrap, like most players do. Noticing another player listening to music on a headset, he remembered he needed some little batteries for his headset.

"Here," somebody said, "take these."

Sometime later he looked in his locker where he thought he had put his new batteries. They weren't there.

"Who," he roared, "stole my batteries?"

The other players didn't know what he was talking about. None of them had even seen his batteries. But all Mickey knew was that his batteries weren't in his locker and now he was really grumbling.

"I know who took 'em," he mumbled. "I know."

"Nobody," he was told, "took your batteries."

By now Mickey had to put on his pads and his uniform and go out for the warm-up. After the warm-up he searched his locker again. No batteries. At halftime, he checked. No batteries. When the game was over, he looked again. No batteries. Still grumbling, he hung up his helmet, took off his jersey and his pants, took off his shoulder pads and all his other pads, then he cut the tape off his ankles and wrists.

When he took off his jockstrap, the batteries fell out.

After I told that story on the air during a Buccaneers–Raiders game, Pat Summerall, as always, had the last word.

"Mickey," he said, "sure was charged up last week."

Stories that good don't come along too often, but when they do, I'm always going to find time to tell them. Football isn't just runs and passes, tackles and blocks, or diagramming a play on the Telestrator. More than anything else, football is people. It's players and coaches. It's the crowd. Every so often you hear some prophet say that years from now there won't be any stadiums, that the games will be played in what amounts to a television studio with no spectators. But if anyone ever believes they don't need the crowd and the crowd noise at the game, then they really don't understand the sport. Or any spectator sport.

You need the crowd. You need its noise. You need its reaction. You need the feeling of a live stadium.

Players need it. Coaches need it. Fans need it. Television needs it. I think the fans being there and making noise and reacting to things are a big part of television. If you had a game with no crowd, no stadium, no noise, you'd just have a big pushing and shoving match. What makes a game go is the crowd and the crowd noise, the fans and their reaction, and the players' and coaches' reactions to the crowd.

All that adds up to the game. And the game is the thing, not me or Pat or the camera angles. The game is what everybody who turns on a TV set is interested in. The game is what I'm interested in.

People are always asking me which team I'm rooting for, but I root for both teams. I really do. I want both teams to do well. I want all the players to do well so that we have a good game to talk about.

The day after we do a game, I check the newspapers to make sure we had everything. Whatever big plays and decisions the coaches and players talk about in the papers, if we had all that in our telecast, that's good. Conversely, if they say this particular play was the turning point and we didn't even mention that, I'd think, *Oh, no, that's terrible.* Or if one of the players said, "In that fourth quarter we were so dead, we couldn't even get in our stances," if we didn't have pictures of that, I'd feel bad. I never want to read about something that happened during the game that we didn't talk about or show.

Once I do a game, I never watch a videotape to see how I did. What I do has to be instinct and reaction. If you start questioning your instincts and your reactions, then you don't do anything. You'll be afraid to make a mistake. You'll be afraid to say the wrong thing.

I'm sure that, just in the shortness of time that's sometimes involved, I've said some things that really didn't make a lot of sense, but maybe they wouldn't have made much sense if I had an hour to say them. Sometimes you're in the middle of saying something, now something else happens and you have to stop your thought and go to what just happened. Or you're developing something about the quarterback and *boom,* he throws an interception. Now the other team has the ball, change of possession. You hear "Ten . . . nine . . . eight . . . commercial." When you come back, the teams have flip-flopped. You've got to go to a new thought.

That's the fun of live television. When you say something, you can't bring it back. You can't edit it. But that's the way I like it.

If you do a feature or a pregame or a commercial, that's a show. The producer or the director can always say, "I didn't like that, let's try it again," or "We had a little glitch with one of our cameras, let's do it over." When you're doing a game, it's not a show. It's live. And when you're live, there's no "do it over." I like the excitement of that.

To me, there's no such thing as a dull game. The person talking about it might be dull. The person watching it might be dull. But if you're playing or coaching in it, it's never dull.

Even when a team is winning by six touchdowns, the fans of that team don't think it's dull. Sometimes in a one-sided game the network will switch to another game that's closer, but the fans of the team that's winning the one-sided game don't want that. Especially if that team was coming off some bad years, like the Cowboys were after their 1–15 record in 1989, Jimmy Johnson's first season as coach. To those fans, a blowout is fun.

I've had fans ask me, "Why did the network switch to that other game? I wanted to see more touchdowns."

So after doing a game, after reading the Monday papers and watching the Monday night game, from Tuesday on I'm preparing for next Sunday's game. Even if I'm doing one of the teams in back-to-back games, I start fresh every week. Once you assume that you know everything about a team, that's when you discover you really don't. Even if I do a Cowboys game back-to-back, it's a different opponent, different circumstances. Coming off a big win or a bad loss.

I check the two teams' news releases, the NFL release and stats, and the newspaper clippings from each team's area. I study the videotapes of each team's last game. And whether I'm home or in a hotel or on the bus, I read the newspapers every day to keep up with not only those two teams but the entire NFL.

No matter what I read, I never circle an item with a red pen to make sure I remember it. I never use notes in the booth. At the University of Oregon a woman professor in a speech class always told us that unless you were giving a speech on science or mathematics where the facts had to be precise, you should never use notes. Her theory was that if you don't know something well enough to talk about it without notes, you shouldn't talk about it in a speech.

To me, if something is important enough, it will stick in my mind. If it's not important, it won't.

Whatever city our game is in, by Friday our Fox team has gathered there—Pat Summerall and me along with Bob Stenner, Sandy Grossman, and all our other production people. Friday or Saturday we always watch film, real coach's game film, at the home team's practice complex. I run it back and forth just like I did when I was coaching. We want to see the offensive blocking schemes and the defensive coverages that the game videotapes never show so that we know what to expect in the game, what to tell our cameramen to look for.

Cameramen are like defensive players. They need to react to the formations, to which players are in the game, to what to expect in certain down-and-yardage situations.

On Saturday we talk to each team's head coach and to some players on each team. We ask the coaches about their starting lineups and about their thinking for this game. I have two questions: "What do you have to do offensively?" and "What do you have to do defensively?" All the answers and the follow-up questions flow from there. After we talk to the coach, we talk to three or four of his players. Over the years I've learned that a player who will be lining up against another player will never tell you how good that other player is. No matter how good each of those players is.

When Steve Wallace was the 49ers' left tackle, he never told me how good Charles Haley was, because Wallace had to build up his own confidence and his dislike for the Cowboys' pass rusher. Conversely, Haley never told me how good Wallace was.

I never want a player to feel I'm interrogating him or cross-examining him. I just want a casual conversation, maybe about something that happened in his last game, anything to keep a conversation going. I don't expect anybody to tell me any secrets. I never ask a coach to tell me something that's off the record because then if I see it, I can't talk about it. But every so often a coach or a player will give me something to look for. Sometimes accidentally. Like the Saturday night at the Cowboys' hotel before their regular-season game in San Francisco in 1994 when Troy Aikman walked into our meeting with his right thumb all taped up.

"What's that?" I said.

Troy told us how he hurt the thumb in practice when he banged it against somebody's helmet as he threw a pass.

"Are you going to play?"

"If the game were today, I couldn't have played," he said. "I can't grip the ball."

"Can you play tomorrow?"

"I hope so," he said.

We didn't know it then, but the Cowboys had not reported Troy's injury to the NFL office. They later were fined $10,000. But Troy never told us not to talk about it. I did a spot on the Fox pregame show explaining the injury. Troy played with the bad thumb. He completed twenty-three of forty-two passes for 339 yards, but he threw three interceptions and the Cowboys lost, 21–14.

Saturday is usually the best day to come up with things like that. I remember once when everybody kept saying that Richard Dent was going to play on Sunday for the Bears, but when we went to practice he was inside riding a bicycle. He didn't play.

Late in the week players will tell you something they might not tell you early in the week. Before the 49ers played the Cowboys in the 1994 NFC championship game in San Francisco, everybody expected Deion Sanders, who was then with the 49ers, to shadow Michael Irvin, the Cowboys' best wide receiver.

"What are you going to do?" I asked Deion. "Stay on one side of the field? Or flip-flop?"

"I'm taking Alvin Harper," he said, meaning the other wide receiver. "I've got Harper."

As soon as the game started, I would've seen that and talked about it, but by knowing it the day before, we went over it in our Saturday night production meeting. We were prepared to cover it better than if it had been a surprise.

Our production meeting, which is held in the crew's hotel, usually lasts two to three hours. Bob Stenner and Sandy Grossman go over everything from the head shots you see of the starting lineups to the trends of each team's offense and defense that our broadcast associates will keep track of.

Before a Packers game, Reggie White told us he would be lining up at different positions on defense: outside the offensive tackle, outside the offensive guard, over the center. So we set up a graphic to illustrate how often he lined up in each spot. As the game progressed, it made for a good graphic.

Before a Giants game, Dan Reeves told us, "We want to get four yards on first down." My rule of thumb is that if you get less than 4 yards on first down, you're likely to need more than 5 yards on third down. So we kept track of what the Giants did on first down: whether they ran or passed and for how many yards. That made another good graphic. But one of Bob Stenner's rules as our producer is, don't overdo statistics.

"I never want stats," Bob often says, "to drive what we put on the air."

Ever since Pat and I teamed up on CBS in 1981 and then moved to Fox in 1994, Bob has been our producer and Sandy Grossman has been our director. As the producer, Bob plans everything. He organizes what players we want to talk to late that week. He checks the practice schedule. He sets up the meeting rooms in our hotel. During the game, Bob is in charge of getting the replays in, getting the commercials in, talking to the Fox people in Hollywood about the halftime show, getting off the air on time, all while Sandy is directing his cameramen. The others on our crew are associate director Rich Russo, broadcast associates Fran Morrison and Mike Roig, stage manager Rich Nelson, statmen Dave Schwalbe and Tom Yohe, and talent spotter Wayne Fidelman.

Believe me, it's as much a team as the Cowboys or the 49ers are. We have to be in sync with each other just as much as Steve Young has to be in sync with Jerry Rice.

Pat and I usually get to a game about three hours before the kickoff, long before the traffic builds up. We sit on the bus for about an hour. Some of the cameramen and technicians will come by and we'll just talk about anything, just hang out. If we're doing the late game, we'll have one of the early games off of the satellite dish. There's always some food. Everybody has something to eat, something to drink.

Sometimes players and coaches stop in. When we're doing a Redskins game, Darrell Green always comes by. When we're doing a Cowboys game, Nate Newton and Charles Haley always do.

About two hours before the game, I change my shirt, put on a tie and my blazer, then Pat and I go up to the booth. Pat and I each have a monitor in front of us. The screen for the Telestrator is to my right. To test it, I just use my forefinger to write "OK," then press the "erase" button. I've got a lineup card in front of me. Behind me are two electric fans to blow the heat from the TV lights out of the booth. Close by are some menthol cough drops in case I need one, and peanuts. Real goobers, real shell peanuts.

Pat and I just throw the shells on the floor of the booth and stand in them. I don't know what it is, but the crunch of those shells just makes the booth feel like it's yours. Sometimes before the game, I'll throw some of the shells out into the stands.

To wash down the peanuts, I always have a big paper cup of lemon juice with honey. If I'm a little congested or a little hoarse, that lemon juice with honey really soothes my throat. I learned about it when I was hosting *Saturday Night Live* in 1982. Jennifer Holliday, the singer who starred on Broadway in *Dreamgirls,* had all these concoctions in her dressing room. One of them was lemon juice with honey.

"Try it," she said.

It tasted good and felt good. I've had it in the booth ever since. One of my bus drivers, Dave Hahn, puts two dozen fresh lemons into an electric squeezer and brings the juice up to the booth where our stage manager, Rich Nelson, spoons a jar of honey into the lemon juice. Except once. When I arrived in our booth at Giants Stadium for a cold late-season game, Pat turned to me.

"John," he said, "the first bulletin from Nellie today was, the honey froze."

I like to get to the booth early just to adjust to looking down at the field. It's a long way down there from even the closest booth, and it's really a long way down from the booths that are up high. I start looking at the benches, at the goal posts, anything to adjust my eyes to the distance. I learned that your eyes can adjust. At least mine can. If you keep looking at something long enough, your eyes will focus themselves to that distance. I don't know if eye doctors would agree with that, but it works for me.

The thing about my eyes, I've never had glasses. I've never had any form of reading problem. I didn't even want to mention that because, knock on wood, tomorrow I'll wake up and I won't be able to see.

Except for rehearsing our opening segment, nothing Pat and I do is formatted. We've been doing this for so many years, if it were ever formatted, if I knew the questions Pat was going to ask or if I had to read an answer off a TelePrompTer, that wouldn't be Pat and that wouldn't be me.

Some announcers in television need everything formatted and if they do, that's fine, that's the way they do it. But the people who do it that way usually can't wing it, just like I can't do the restrictive stuff.

I always have binoculars with me but I seldom use them. During the warm-up or just before the game I'll put my binoculars on a certain player to see if he's wearing a bandage or a cast or a brace. That way, when he's on the screen later, I've seen it before. During the game I'll only use my binoculars to check on a player who's down because he's injured or to check the huddle during a change of possession to make sure the players are the same players. If there's a new quarterback or if Emmitt Smith is out or Jerry Rice is out, I'll know that right away but if there's a new tackle I might not notice him. So every change of possession I look in the huddle and go down the line, *boom, boom, boom, boom, boom,* everyone's there. Or if they're not, I'll realize that, say, Jumbo Elliott, the Jets' big offensive tackle, isn't there. When we come back from the commercial, we'll get a picture of Jumbo on the sideline and we'll mention it.

Down in the truck, Bob and Sandy are putting everything together with the crew and the cameramen. Bob is on the phone to the Fox studios, Sandy is talking to his cameramen, others are checking the switches. In front of Sandy are six rows of small screens (some of them black), two big screens, one big monitor, one smaller monitor, and dozens of little keys and switches and lights. If you put a big enough rocket on that truck, you could go to the moon.

When a commercial is on during a time-out I can talk into my microphone to Sandy without it going out over the air. I might say, "Let's show Jerry Rice moving off the line," or "Darrell Green is going everywhere Michael Irvin is." But in my earpiece I'll hear Rich Russo, our associate director, yelling, "Ten seconds . . . nine . . . eight . . ." That's when I stop talking to Sandy because we're about to go back on the air.

Pat and I each have a monitor in front of us, but when the game is on, I don't watch the monitor. I watch the play, I watch the field, I watch everything. But after the play is over, I watch the monitor because now I've got to talk about what's on the monitor. When the play was going on, Pat was talking, I wasn't. I was watching everything. When the play is over, now I either saw something, and I start talking about it and they give me a replay; or if, say, Jay Novacek made a great catch, I'll hear "isolate" in my headset. That means they have Jay isolated. I know I'm going to get an isolate replay of Jay from the truck where Sandy Grossman has as many as twelve different pictures on twelve different screens in front of him.

Before the replay, nobody tells me what happened. I've got to know what happened. All I hear is "replay, end zone" or "replay, sideline" or "replay, pit," meaning the view of the offensive and defensive lines from the line of scrimmage.

Every so often, if a running back gets hit and you know he fumbled but you haven't seen the ball come out, I might hear, "We've got another angle where you see the ball come out." On something like that, you do know what's coming. If I feel I have to talk to Sandy about something, I can push the "cough" key and talk to him. But there's very little talking between us. You don't have time to be talking to the viewers on the air and listening for Bob or Sandy at the same time. That can be very distracting. Sometimes when I'm watching tapes of other games, I can tell when an announcer is listening to the voice in his headset.

Pat and I have been working with Bob and Sandy for so long that we don't need to talk much during a game. Like any four workmen on the same job for any length of time, you start thinking alike. You just say a word and the other guys know what you're talking about.

Every so often I'll see something happen that I want to talk about when there's no picture of it, but if Sandy's got something else on the screen, I'll back off. It's whoever gets there first. If Sandy gets there first with the picture, I talk about his picture. And if I start talking about something else, Sandy will find a picture to go with it. If the quarterback had plenty of time to throw, if I say, "You've got to give credit to the offensive line on that one," Sandy will come up with a picture of the offensive line blocking the pass rushers. Neither of us is trying to be first. It's just how the flow goes. If Sandy gets there first with a replay, I don't talk about something else. Talking about something the viewer can't see is the worst thing an analyst can do. When the pictures are there on the screen, you talk about the pictures on the screen.

Diagramming a play on the Telestrator is tricky, but the actual diagram is easier. I used to have to draw it on the monitor with a pen, but now I just do it with my finger, then later I push the "erase" button.

I know what I'm going to see when the picture comes up, but it's tricky when the picture is from behind the end zone. You only have a camera in one end zone, but every quarter the teams flip which way they're going. It's just a little thing, but if the end-zone camera is behind the 49ers and we're trying to show Russell Maryland, the Raiders' defensive tackle, on a matchup with Jesse Sapolu, the 49ers' guard, I can't see Russell because the whole 49ers offense is between him and the guy who's down. So that's a bad time to show a defense.

If the end-zone camera is behind the 49ers' offense, you can show what their offensive line is doing. You can see Jesse Sapolu pulling or tackle Harris Barton blocking down.

No matter what play you're diagramming, you have to know where everyone is. That's why I study film so much. If we're doing a Steelers game, you know Rod Woodson is the left cornerback on first down, but when the Steelers go to a nickel defense, he moves inside over the slotback. When you're looking to circle Woodson on the Telestrator, if you're looking for him out there on that left corner, you'll never find him. You have to know how they play and where they play. Some guys are always moving around, like Reggie White and Charles Haley. That's why I watch so much film. I don't have time to look for a player's number. I've got to be able to recognize a player's body.

I've been doing games since 1979, but I really don't know what Bob Stenner, Sandy Grossman, and everybody else in the truck go through during a game. I'm never down there in the truck during a game.

I see all the wires and plugs and stuff on that big truck on my way into the stadium and on my way out, and I always wonder, *What if somebody just pulled the plug?* My bus even got accused of that once. When we do a Bears game at Soldier Field in Chicago, they let my bus park parallel to our television truck. But during a game there a few years ago the Telestrator wasn't working right.

"It's your bus's fault," somebody said.

"My bus's fault! How can it be my bus's fault?"

"Your bus ran over one of the cables."

Hey, I'm not so sure anybody knew, but I didn't know either. Maybe my bus was to blame. Now every time we do a game at Soldier Field, I tell everybody to check to make sure my bus isn't parked near the cables. Another time in the Oakland Coliseum our booth was really a basket. The stadium was still being used for baseball, so the football field went from home plate to centerfield instead of from first base to third base. To put us on the 50-yard line, they built a temporary booth out of a basket and hung us out there.

Some things belong in a basket, like fruit and flowers and babies. Some things don't belong in a basket. I don't belong in a basket.

But if I had to do every game from a basket, I'd do it. I can't think of anything I'd rather do than what I do. If I could, I'd do it forever.